LIBRARY SKILLS

A GUIDEBOOK FOR INTRODUCING

LIBRARY SKILLS

TO

KINDERGARTEN & PRIMARY GRADES

By

MARGARET V. BECK

Elementary School Librarian, Austin, Minnesota

B.S., St. Cloud State College, St. Cloud, Minnesota

M.A., University of Denver, Denver, Colorado

and

VERA M. PACE

Elementary School Librarian, Austin, Minnesota

B.A., State College of Iowa, Cedar Falls, Iowa

M.A., University of Minnesota, Minneapolis, Minnesota

PUBLISHERS

T. S. DENISON & COMPANY, INC.

MINNEAPOLIS

Copyright ©, 1967, by

T. S. DENISON & COMPANY, INC.

First Printing—December 1967
Second Printing—April 1968
Third Printing—August 1968
Fourth Printing—December 1968
Fifth Printing—June 1969
Sixth Printing—November 1969

Printed in the U.S.A.

BY THE BRINGS PRESS

International Copyright Secured

Library of Congress Catalog Card Number: 64-7704

CONTENTS

INTRODUCTION

The purposes of the LIBRARY SKILLS series are twofold:

1. To arouse a lasting interest in authors and books and an appreciation for the library as a prime resource in the search for knowledge.

2. To lay the groundwork for intelligent library usage through the systematic teaching of the library skills needed co carry out effectively the elementary school program.

A GUIDEBOOK FOR INTRODUCING LIBRARY SKILLS TO KINDERGARTEN AND PRIMARY GRADES aids the librarian or classroom teacher in organizing a library program that will stimulate interest in and an appreciation for books and the services the library offers students in the elementary school.

Book One, LIBRARY SKILLS—USING THE CARD CATALOG, is the foundation for acquiring the skills that lead toward more independent use of the library.

Book Two, LIBRARY SKILLS—USING THE DEWEY DECIMAL SYSTEM, goes a step further by presenting the orderly arrangement of nonfiction books according to the Dewey Decimal System of Classification which is presented in its basic form.

Book Three, LIBRARY SKILLS—USING REFERENCE MATERIAL guides the elementary school student in using the library for beginning research.

The program outlined by the series can be carried out under the direction of either teacher or librarian. It lends itself to cooperative teaching by both.

To be used most effectively, the procedures outlined in the GUIDES should be carefully followed. The GUIDE presents the proper sequence of instruction to be followed to insure understanding. Check-up exercises for Books One, Two and Three are provided to help keep the teacher or librarian informed of the extent of the student's understanding of ideas presented before introducing a new idea. The GUIDES also give a wide variety of suggestions to enrich the library program and stimulate children's interest in reading.

Library instruction is an ongoing, developmental process. No one grade level is ideal for the teaching of any particular skill. For this reason it is necessary for the teacher and librarian to be prepared to meet different levels of readiness.

The examination of the title page begins with the kindergarten sharing of a picture book and is built up to its more refined use as a source of information for a sixth grade bibliographic entry.

The sections of the library may be introduced to individuals at any grade level when they show an interest in or a need for information in books other than those found in the picture book collection.

The use of the card catalog should be started at any time when a child shows a need for such instruction. The ideas suggested in LIBRARY SKILLS—BOOK ONE may well serve to guide an able second or third grade student in mastering this skill.

The foundations for using the reference section are begun as early as kindergarten when the teacher or librarian uses the dictionary or the encyclopedia to answer questions that arise. By instructing small groups in the use of reference books at a time when they have a real desire to learn how to use them is the best possible motivation. The keeping of library book reading records may begin with the teacher in kindergarten preparing a chart to which she adds the picture books that she shares with her class and may continue through the grade levels to those kept by individuals with a personal evaluation added.

It is important to keep children informed on the added features of the public library to which they can turn for additional help.

A SUGGESTED PLAN FOR LIBRARY INSTRUCTION
IN THE ELEMENTARY GRADES

KINDERGARTEN:

Introduction to the library and to the librarian.
Care of books.
Enjoyment of books.

FIRST GRADE:

Library procedures.
Selecting books.
Checking out books.
Returning books.
Home care of books.
Appreciation of books.
Develop an awareness of proper library conduct.
Incidental instruction on parts of a title page.

SECOND GRADE:

Review and continued emphasis on previous instruction.

Extend appreciation of books through introduction of books by specific authors and illustrators.

Introduce Caldecott Award winners.

Introduce the Fiction section through books by Haywood.

THIRD GRADE:

Review of all previous instruction.

Continue to present books by specific authors with less emphasis on the work of illustrators and more on story content and author's background for writing.

Greater individual guidance, with help for those able to read more difficult material.

Sharing of ideas through book discussions.

Introduce the two main parts of the library: Fiction and Nonfiction.

Special lessons on each of the following parts of the Nonfiction section of the library: Fairy Tales, Science, Biography, Poetry.

FOURTH GRADE:

Continuation of previous instruction.

How to use the library card catalog.

Practice in using the card catalog to locate books when only the author is known; when only the title is known; when books on a specific subject are needed.

Parts of a book emphasizing index and table of contents.

Arrangement of biography books.

Encourage the keeping of individual reading records.

Appreciation and enjoyment of books through introduction of authors, introduction of illustrators, book discussions.

FIFTH GRADE:

Review of all previous instruction.

Introduce the Dewey Decimal System of Classification.

Relate the Dewey Decimal System from the call number on the catalog card to the book on the shelf.

Present tall tales as typical American humor.

Correlate the library program with the social studies curriculum.

Build an appreciation of authors who try to give their readers a better understanding of people, places, and events past and present in the United States.

Encourage the keeping of a reading record.

SIXTH GRADE:

Review of all skills presented thus far.

Introduce materials for reference work.

Teach the making of a bibliography.

Introduce the Newbery Award books and the runners-up and encourage the reading of these "honor" books.

Prepare for the transition to the Junior High School Library by introducing a more detailed Dewey Decimal System and more detailed card catalog through use of film strips and discussion.

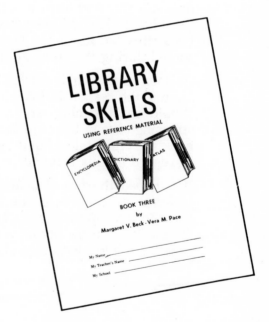

KINDERGARTEN

A successful introduction to the library in the kindergarten is of the greatest importance. These first impressions and habits will be the building blocks for future lessons. Here is the opportunity to provide the reason for wanting to learn to read, the chance to build a common background of books shared that may become a part of the children's everyday living in the classroom. The borrowing of books presents a real-life situation involving respect and responsibility for public property at home as well as at school.

The teacher introduces the children to the librarian and the librarian introduces them to the library and the picture book collection. The children soon discover that the librarian is an expert on books who can help them find books about characters and on topics of special interest to them.

During library periods with the kindergarten class the librarian discusses the care and handling of books, the arrangement of the picture books in their special section, and library manners (citizenship). Story hours and browsing periods form a major part of the kindergarten program in the library. Old favorites, new books, holiday and seasonal stories, and books related to classroom units are introduced. The children share the delight of the wonderful picture book illustrations as the best in books for children their age is presented during the story hour.

As soon as the kindergarten teacher feels the children are ready to assume the responsibility of caring for a library book, the librarian should aid the children in choosing books for home circulation, stressing care of books in the home. A letter accompanying the first book the child takes home will explain what is expected of parents in regard to this privilege.

It is hoped the fun of hearing stories and enjoying pictures in the pleasant atmosphere of the library will lead children to a desire to learn to read. With the librarian rests the responsibility for making the weekly library period a most anticipated and enjoyable experience for the kindergarten class.

A VISIT TO THE LIBRARY

Purpose:

To introduce the librarian and the room called "the library" to the kindergarten class.

Materials Needed:

Bulletin board displays planned for this occasion.

Attractive copies of "old favorites" displayed.

> The Tale of Peter Rabbit
> The Three Bears
> The Three Little Pigs
> Three Billy Goats Gruff
> Several Mother Goose books

A new book—a story not known by the children.

The Class Session:

This important introduction to the library should be carefully planned so that it will be a pleasant and memorable occasion.

The entire library must look inviting as the librarian welcomes the children into the room where wonderful story and picture books may be found.

As the children take a guided tour about the room they will be awed by the many books on the shelves and delighted to find an area ready and waiting for them where they can sit quietly to hear a story and enjoy the pictures from a new book.

Point out the appearance of the pretty new book with pride and stress the importance of clean hands to keep books looking like new for a long time.

Enjoy the story.

Call attention to the way you turned pages from the top, preventing the tears that happen when pages are improperly turned from the bottom.

Challenge the children to remember these two important rules—clean hands and proper turning of the pages—when they look at books at home or in the kindergarten room or in the library.

Dismiss the class with an invitation to return another day to hear another story.

Follow-up:

Teacher-librarian cooperation in teaching children to handle books properly.

Children may each bring a book from home to make a library in the kindergarten room.

ARRANGEMENT OF THE PICTURE BOOK SECTION

Purpose:

To acquaint the kindergarten children with the picture book section and to give them an opportunity to browse in this section.

Materials Needed:

A mounted storybook character or nursery rhyme character to be placed one at each table.

> or

A different colored square, circle or triangle at each table and the book, WING ON A FLEA, by Emberly. Little.

The Class Session:

For the purpose of class organization, each table may have a mounted familiar storybook character or nursery rhyme character placed in the center of the table.

Point out to the children the extent of the picture book section, these books being their special books. Explain that the books belong in their special "bins" or "houses."

Going to the picture book shelves, take a book from the shelf and hold it before the class. Point to the title on the front of the book as you read it aloud. Show the children the spine of the book and read the title from the book's spine. Demonstrate how books should be returned to their right "bins" or "houses" with their spines showing so the book's title can be seen. Turn the book around and show how the book looks when it is not put back properly. Then as all watch, place the book back in its proper place with the spine showing.

Recall the rules about clean hands and proper turning of pages. Remind the children that you will be watching for boys and girls who have learned these two important rules as they look at books in the library today.

"Now we have two new rules:

We put books back in their own houses and we put each book back so its name or title will show."

Select several books at random. Tell a little about each story and demonstrate how you turn the pages from the top as you show a few pictures, and then very carefully return the book to its proper place on the shelf with its spine showing.

Call children by tables ("The boys and girls at the Peter Rabbit table") to go to the shelves and to sit down in front of a "bin" or "house" and look through some of the books.

> (An alternate plan for organizing the class may be to use colored paper squares, circles and triangles, one on each table. The children will enjoy hearing THE WING ON A FLEA read to them before they are given directions for going to the shelves by tables. This book is about colored rectangles, squares, circles and triangles. The tables may be called by shapes and colors. "The boys and girls at the 'red circle table' may go to the shelves.")

Use the first group called to set an example.

"I like the way these boys and girls are showing us they know the book rules. I like the way they turn the pages from the top. I see them returning their books to the proper places and the spines are showing. Good, you remembered!"

Proceed to call other tables to go to the shelves. Walk behind the children, complimenting them on remembering rules and making comments about the books they are discovering.

After the children have spent a little time enjoying the pictures in the books in front of them, call them back to their tables one at a time.

Follow-up:

This plan or a similar plan for browsing should be carried out by the librarian or the classroom teacher for several library periods.

For variation: After the children become familiar with the proper places for the books, each may be allowed to select a book and return to his table. After looking at the book for a minute or two the teacher or librarian might ask that each person pass the book to the person on his right. This should proceed until the person gets his own book choice back. Then the children should be excused by tables to return their books to the proper place. Several children may be chosen to walk along the picture book shelving to see that books are returned with the spine showing.

THE KINDERGARTEN CHILD SELECTS A BOOK

Purpose:

To give each kindergarten child a chance to select a book of his own choosing to take to the kindergarten room.

Materials Needed:

The book, TELL ME SOME MORE, by Crosby Bonsall. Harper. An introduction to the library, a place where you can hold an elephant or a camel in your hand—in a book!

A collection of about six books, one each about an elephant, a camel, a lion, a hippopotamus, a giraffe, or any wild or domestic animal.

Chairs arranged in a story circle.

The Class Session:

The story circle is ready and waiting when the kindergarten class arrives and they are invited to find chairs in the circle.

Recall past visits to the library.

"Our story today is about two friends, Tim and Andrew. As the story begins they are talking together."

Read the story.

Following the reading of the story, bring out, one by one, the books about a lion, an elephant, a hippopotamus, etc. Share together the same kind of fun Tim and Andrew had as they walked home from the library.

"Today we have a special treat! You may each choose a book to take back to the kindergarten room."

Recall book care rules.

Explain the charging system briefly.

"These books will be signed out in your teacher's name. I will write your teacher's name on the book card."

"I wonder what you will carry back to the room with you today to surprise your teacher!"

Instruct the children to bring the books they select to the charging desk where you will check them out to the kindergarten teacher.

Follow-up:

In the classroom the children will enjoy sharing the books they have selected with their teacher as each one demonstrates how strong he is as he carries a heavy load easily—in a book! As each child has his turn to demonstrate what he can carry, the teacher will probably say, "Tell me some more!" as she calls on each child in turn.

SELECTING THE FIRST BOOK TO TAKE HOME

Purpose:

To turn the responsibility for book care over to each child as parents join the teacher and librarian in teaching care of books and in encouraging appreciation and enjoyment of books.

Materials Needed:

Each child must be ready with a plastic bag in which to carry his book to and from school. His name should be clearly marked on the bag.

Book Care posters made by the librarian on 9" x 12" paper.

Letters to parents.

Class list.

The Class Session:

The children will enjoy recalling library and book rules as the librarian shares with them the following posters.

We use quiet voices in the library.

17

Clean hands.

We turn pages from the top.

We carry books to and from home
in a plastic bag.

After looking at books, we return them to their proper places.

We will find a safe place to keep our books at home when we are not looking at them.

"Today is a very special day. I believe you are ready to take a book home to share with your family. You know the book rules and you have your plastic bags all ready to carry your book safely to and from home. Each of you has thought of a safe place to keep your book when you are not looking at it."

Review the charging system.

"Today I will put your name on the card for the book you choose to take home. I will stamp a date on the card and on the date due slip in the book. This tells you and your family when the book must be returned to the library."

"As you have your book checked out I will put this letter to Mom and Dad in the book pocket. This letter tells them about our library and about library books. It tells them what to do if a book is accidentally damaged while you have it checked out in your name. The letter tells them not to mend a torn or damaged book, but to return the book to school where it will be mended with special mending material by a person who is an expert in mending books."

Suggested aids to assist the librarian in checking out books to kindergarten children:

Each child may wear a name tag.

With a class list handy, the children may tell the librarian their names with the list used to help with spelling.

The librarian may have printed each child's name from the class list on cards that are handed to the children before they leave the story circle or tables to select their books. They present these cards as they bring their book to the desk.

If the plastic bags are clearly marked, the children may bring their bags to the desk and show their names as they check out their books.

Following the reading of the book, WHAT'S YOUR NAME? by Zhenya Gay, Viking, the librarian may make a game of asking, "What's your name?"

Back in the story circle or at the tables with their books along with their letters to their parents, in their plastic bags, the kindergarten children are told that they are responsible now for proper care of the library book they have selected. Each child grows up a little as he assumes his new responsibility—to care for a library book.

A LETTER TO PARENTS

Dear Parents:

Today I am bringing home a book from our school library. I can keep it for **one** week. Will you help me with these things?—

1. Read the book with me and let me tell you about the pictures.

2. Help me find a place where I can keep my library book so it will not get lost or damaged.

3. Remind me to have clean hands when I read, and to turn my pages from the upper right-hand corner.

4. Send the book back to the library to be mended if it is accidentally damaged while it is charged out to me.

5. Have a small plastic bag for me to use when I carry my book home and back to school each week.

Thank you for helping me. I think it's lots of fun to read with you.

Love,

STORY HOURS AND BROWSING PERIODS

Purpose:

To stimulate children's interest in books.

To help in developing good listening habits.

To help build an appreciation for good literature.

To introduce many books, new and old, to stimulate imagination, to give information, to enjoy the illustrations, and to help build a common background.

Materials Needed:

Books

Filmstrips

Recordings

Puppets

Flannelboard and storybook figures

Simple costumes: cape, crown, cane, hats, etc.

The Class Session:

Stories may be introduced in the library through a number of methods. Reading the story or telling the story while showing the pictures is the most simple and still very effective method. Filmstrips and recordings may be used. Hand puppets add interest to storytelling as does the use of the flannelboard.

Follow-up:

Creative dramatics using simple costuming.

Puppet plays.

Retelling of stories by the children.

Illustrating the "best part."

Relating incidents in the classroom to like incidents from books shared.

Books every kindergarten child should have the privilege of knowing:

Favorite Book Characters:

THE STORY OF LITTLE BLACK SAMBO	Bannerman (Lippincott)
GEORGIE stories	Bright (Doubleday)
JOHNNY CROW stories	Brooke (Warne)
KATY AND THE BIG SNOW	Burton (Houghton)
MIKE MULLIGAN AND HIS STEAM SHOVEL	
THE LITTLE HOUSE	
THE HAPPY LION stories	Fatio (McGraw)
ANGUS books	Flack (Doubleday)
THE STORY ABOUT PING	
JEANNE-MARIE stories	Francoise (Scribner)
LITTLE TOOT	Gramatky (Putnam)

HAROLD AND THE PURPLE CRAYON stories	Johnson (Harper)
MARSHMALLOW	Newberry (Harper)
KATY NO-POCKET	Payne (Houghton)
THE TALE OF BENJAMIN BUNNY	Potter (Warne)
THE TALE OF PETER RABBIT	
CURIOUS GEORGE stories	Rey (Houghton)
ANATOLE stories	Titus (McGraw)
THE BIGGEST BEAR	Ward (Houghton)
HARRY THE DIRTY DOG stories	Zion (Harper)

_____   _____

_____   _____

_____   _____

_____   _____

_____   _____

_____   _____

Stories for Seasons and Holidays:

AUTUMN:

Beim	ANDY AND THE SCHOOL BUS. Morrow
Lenski	NOW IT'S FALL. Walck
	A DOG GOES TO SCHOOL. Walck
McCloskey	BLUEBERRIES FOR SAL. Viking
Tresselt	AUTUMN HARVEST. Lothrop
	JOHNNY MAPLE LEAF. Lothrop

_____   _____

_____   _____

_____   _____

_____   _____

HALLOWEEN:

Bright   GEORGIE'S HALLOWEEN. Doubleday
Tudor   PUMPKIN MOONSHINE. Walck

_____   _____

_____   _____

_____   _____

THANKSGIVING:

Dalgliesh   THE THANKSGIVING STORY. Scribner

_____   _____

_____   _____

WINTER:

Burton   KATY AND THE BIG SNOW. Houghton
Hader   THE BIG SNOW. Macmillan
Keats   THE SNOWY DAY. Viking
Krauss   THE HAPPY DAY. Harper
Lindgren   THE TOMTEN. Coward-McCann
Tresselt   WHITE SNOW, BRIGHT SNOW. Lothrop

_____   _____

_____   _____

_____   _____

_____   _____

CHRISTMAS:

Adshead	BROWNIES—IT'S CHRISTMAS. Walck
Anglund	CHRISTMAS IS A TIME OF GIVING. Harcourt
Baker	THE FRIENDLY BEASTS. Parnassus
Brown	SOMETHING FOR CHRISTMAS. Harper
Duvoisin	THE CHRISTMAS WHALE. Knopf
Francoise	NOEL FOR JEANNE-MARIE. Scribner
Janice	LITTLE BEAR'S CHRISTMAS. Lothrop
Joslin	BABY ELEPHANT AND THE SECRET WISHES. Harcourt
Lindgren	CHRISTMAS IN THE STABLE. Coward-McCann
Tudor	THE DOLL'S CHRISTMAS. Walck

_____   _____

_____   _____

_____   _____

_____   _____

SPRING:

Anglund	SPRING IS A NEW BEGINNING. Harcourt
Bright	MY RED UMBRELLA. Morrow
Ets	GILBERTO AND THE WIND. Viking
Fish	WHEN THE ROOT CHILDREN WAKE UP. Lippincott
Francoise	THE BIG RAIN. Scribner
	SPRINGTIME FOR JEANNE-MARIE. Scribner
Kingman	PETER'S LONG WALK. Doubleday
Lenski	SPRING IS HERE. Walck
Schlein	LITTLE RED NOSE. Abelard-Schuman
Tresselt	FOLLOW THE WIND. Lothrop
	HI, MR. ROBIN! Lothrop
Wiese	FISH IN THE AIR. Viking
Yashima	UMBRELLA. Viking
Zolotow	THE STORM BOOK. Harper

_____   _____

_____   _____

_____   _____

_____   _____

EASTER:

Brown	CHEERFUL. Harper
Heyward	THE COUNTRY BUNNY AND THE LITTLE GOLD SHOES. Houghton
Wiese	HAPPY EASTER. Viking

_____   _____

_____   _____

_____   _____

_____   _____

SUMMER:

Lenski	ON A SUMMER DAY. Walck
Tresselt	SUN UP. Lothrop
Udry	THE MOON JUMPERS. Harper
	A TREE IS NICE. Harper
Zion	THE PLANT SITTER. Harper
	HARRY BY THE SEA. Harper

_____   _____

_____   _____

_____   _____

_____   _____

_____   _____

_____   _____

CHANGING SEASONS:

Burton	THE LITTLE HOUSE. Houghton
Duvoisin	THE HOUSE OF FOUR SEASONS. Lothrop
Tudor	AROUND THE YEAR. Walck
Zolotow	OVER AND OVER. Harper

_____   _____

_____   _____

_____   _____

_____   _____

ALL KINDS OF ANIMALS:

De Regniers	MAY I BRING A FRIEND? Atheneum
Duvoisin	A FOR THE ARK. Lothrop
Ets	ANOTHER DAY. Viking
	IN THE FOREST. Viking
	JUST ME. Viking
	PLAY WITH ME. Viking
Fischer	THE BIRTHDAY. Harcourt
	PITSCHI. Harcourt
Flack	ASK MR. BEAR. Macmillan
Garelick	WHERE DOES THE BUTTERFLY GO WHEN IT RAINS? Scott
Garten	THE ALPHABET TALE. Random
Gay	LOOK. Viking
	WHAT'S YOUR NAME? Viking
Ipcar	BROWN COW FARM. Doubleday
	I LOVE ANIMALS. Knopf
Lathrop	WHO GOES THERE? Macmillan
Lenski	ANIMALS FOR ME. Walck
Munari	BRUNO MUNARI'S ZOO. World
Rojankovsky	ANIMALS IN THE ZOO. World
Seuss	IF I RAN THE ZOO. Random
Williams	THE BIG GOLDEN ANIMAL ABC. Golden

28

FAVORITE STORIES:

Brooke	GOLDEN GOOSE BOOK. Warne
Grimm	SHOEMAKER AND THE ELVES. Scribner
Lefevre	THE COCK, THE MOUSE AND THE LITTLE RED HEN. Macrae-Smith
McCloskey	MAKE WAY FOR DUCKLINGS. Viking
Sendak	WHERE THE WILD THINGS ARE. Harper

_____   _____

_____   _____

_____   _____

_____   _____

_____   _____

BOOKS AND MUSIC:

Gag	ABC BUNNY. Coward-McCann
Iviney	COMPLETE VERSION OF YE THREE BLIND MICE. Warne
Langstaff	FROG WENT A COURTIN'. Harcourt
	OL' DAN TUCKER. Harcourt
	OVER IN THE MEADOW. Harcourt
	THE SWAPPING BOY. Harcourt
Nic Leodhas	ALWAYS ROOM FOR ONE MORE. Holt
Robbins	BABOUSHKA AND THE THREE KINGS. Parnassus
Schackburg	YANKEE DOODLE. Prentice-Hall
Spier (illus.)	FOX WENT OUT ON A CHILLY NIGHT. Doubleday

_____   _____

_____   _____

_____   _____

_____   _____

FOR CREATIVE DRAMATICS AND PUPPET PLAYS:

Anglund	NIBBLE NIBBLE MOUSEKIN. Harcourt
Brown (illus.)	THE THREE BILLY GOATS GRUFF. Harcourt
Brown (illus.)	STONE SOUP. Scribner
Grimm	THE WOLF AND THE SEVEN LITTLE KIDS. Harcourt
Grimm	THE HARE AND THE TORTOISE. McGraw
Kepes	LADY BIRD, QUICKLY. Little
Lenski	THE LITTLE AUTO. Walck
Lenski	PAPA SMALL. Walck
Galdone (illus.)	OLD WOMAN AND HER PIG. McGraw
Galdone (illus.)	OLD MOTHER HUBBARD AND HER DOG. McGraw
Tresselt	THE MITTEN. Lothrop

_____   _____

_____   _____

_____   _____

_____   _____

_____   _____

VERY SPECIAL EDITIONS OF MOTHER GOOSE:

BRIAN WILDSMITH'S MOTHER GOOSE. Watts

IN A PUMPKIN SHELL. Illus. Joan Walsh Anglund. Harcourt

MARGUERITE de ANGELI'S A POCKET FULL OF POSIES. Doubleday

MOTHER GOOSE: Seventy-seven Verses With Pictures by Tasha Tudor. Walck

THE REAL MOTHER GOOSE, illus. Blanche Fisher Wright. Rand

RING O' ROSES, illus. L. Leslie Brooke. Warne

THE TALL BOOK OF MOTHER GOOSE, illus. Feodor Rojankovsky. Harper

FILMSTRIPS FOR THE KINDERGARTEN CLASS:

From Weston Woods, Weston, Conn. 06883

Ardizonne	LITTLE TIM AND THE BRAVE SEA CAPTAIN
Bright	GEORGIE
Burton	MIKE MULLIGAN AND HIS STEAM SHOVEL
Daugherty	ANDY AND THE LION
Duvoisin	PETUNIA
Ets	PLAY WITH ME
Ets	IN THE FOREST
Flack	THE STORY ABOUT PING
Flack	ANGUS AND THE DUCKS

Freeman	NORMAN THE DOORMAN
Gag	MILLIONS OF CATS
Gramatky	LITTLE TOOT
Keats	THE SNOWY DAY
Keats	WHISTLE FOR WILLIE
Lindgren	CHRISTMAS IN THE STABLE
Lindgren	THE TOMTEN
McCloskey	BLUEBERRIES FOR SAL
McCloskey	MAKE WAY FOR DUCKLINGS
Potter	THE TALE OF PETER RABBIT
Rey	CURIOUS GEORGE RIDES A BIKE
Slobodkin	MAGIC MICHAEL
Udry	A TREE IS NICE
Will	FINDERS KEEPERS

_____   _____

_____   _____

_____   _____

_____   _____

_____   _____

FIRST GRADE

The first grade child has been properly introduced to the library as a place where he can find help in selecting books to meet his needs and satisfy his interests. He now is ready to assume responsibility for following accepted library procedures such as signing his own book card and proper care of books checked out in his name as well as acceptable conduct during library visits. Because of a rich background of shared book experiences in the kindergarten, he is now ready to become acquainted with new book friends through an introduction to books by an author, an illustrator, or by a topic.

Since he is now learning to read, he wants assistance in finding books that he can read as well as other books that he wants to look at and have read to him. Experiences with books should lead first grade children to a continuing desire to learn to read for enjoyment and information.

BORROWING BOOKS

Purpose:

To instruct children in the library's system of charging or lending books.

To develop a growing sense of personal responsibility for the care of books.

Materials Needed:

A library book with a book card in the pocket.

A practice book card.

Duplicate the following facsimile:

E **B**		
AUTHOR Bergey		
TITLE Rocky, the rocket mouse		
DATE DUE	BORROWER'S NAME	ROOM NUMBER

The Class Session:

This lesson may be carried out by the teacher in the classroom.

Each child is given a duplicated "book card." The librarian or teacher opens a library book and shows the book card in its pocket. The children are told that the book card printed on the paper handed them is similar to the card in the library book.

Point out and read the title of the book and the author's name from the children's "book card."

The children should be made to feel that they are assuming a responsibility that shows they are growing up when they sign for a library book. They are promising as good citizens to care for the book they are borrowing from the school's library.

Guide the children in finding the first line on the practice card. Explain the importance of using only one line. This is important for first grade children generally use two spaces for writing their names. Explain the reason for not skipping a line. Have the children fill in their names and room number or grade in the proper space on the first line, in the first space. Have them pass the card on to their neighbor. Instruct the second child signing the card to sign on the very next line. Continue in this manner while checking to see that the children are using only one space, are not skipping spaces, and are filling in the information required properly. Have the children pass the cards along until all spaces are filled. Now explain that on a real card the next person would turn the card over and write on the space at the top of the back of the card. Explain what is done in your library when the card is completely filled.

Stress the importance of returning books to the place provided in the library since the books cannot be shelved until the cards are put back in them. Every book on the shelf should have a card in its pocket. Explain what might happen if a book is not returned to the place designated as the book return. (The person who last checked out the book may get a notice that the book has not been returned to the library because the card is still in the box and not in the book.)

Follow-up:

Each child assumes the responsibility of signing his name to the book cards of the books he borrows from the library collection.

A LETTER TO PARENTS

Dear Parents:

You can help your first grade reader.

1. Help your child to select books of concern to him.

2. Encourage him when selecting books to take notice of the illustrations.

3. Help your child find a place for his library book out of reach of the family pet and little brothers and sisters.

4. Remind your child to return books on time.

5. Help your child find a good place to read—good light is important.

6. Enjoy books with your child. Have fun discussing the parts of the story he liked best.

7. Really listen to him when he reads to you.

8. When your child reads, help him with proper names and uncommon words when he asks.

9. Let your child see you reading for enjoyment.

10. Ask his teacher or librarian for suggestions of ways to encourage your young reader and for help in choosing books to read to him or to purchase for his home library.

_____

Your Child's Librarian

P.S. Remember to send any library books accidentally damaged to school for repair. Do not mend library books at home.

RESPONSIBLE CITIZENSHIP

Purpose:

To stress care of library books.

To stress the responsibility of each child in the care and handling of library books.

Materials Needed:

Posters (librarian-made or made by the children).

Bookmarks stressing book care designed by Hardie Gramatky. Order from: Children's Book Council, Inc., 175 Fifth Avenue, New York, New York. $1.50 per 100.

Damaged books.

The Class Session:

Have a display of damaged books. Through discussion have the children determine how the book could have received such damage.

Review rules discussed when the children were in kindergarten. The librarian may want to use the same posters that were used in presenting the rules on book care to the kindergarten classes. Children enjoy the return to the familiar.

Present the bookmark. Give one to each child. Have the children look at the "Don't" side of the bookmark.

"The book is telling us some things we must never do when we are looking at or reading a book."

DON'T put fingerprints on my pages.

DON'T bend my pages.

DON'T open me roughly or set me down on my pages.

DON'T turn my pages from the bottom.

"On the other side of the bookmark are some reminders of things we should do."

PROTECT ME FROM . . .

Wet weather

Dogs

Babies

And for remembering all these things, the books say:

THANKS!

"As you use this marker it will remind you of the important book-care rules."

Follow-up:

The children may enjoy making book-care posters that may be displayed in the library.

CATS HERE, CATS THERE, CATS AND KITTENS EVERYWHERE

Purpose:

To guide children in appreciation of a variety of stories and illustrations on one subject: cats.

Materials Needed:

Books to Share With the Class:

Averill	THE FIRE CAT. Harper
Birnbaum	GREEN EYES. Capitol Pub.
Brown, Marcia	FELICE. Scribner
Chalmers	TAKE A NAP, HARRY. Harper
	THROW A KISS, HARRY. Harper
(Unknown)	DAME WIGGINS OF LEE AND HER SEVEN WONDERFUL CATS. McGraw
Fischer	PITSCHI. Harcourt
Flack	ANGUS AND THE CAT. Doubleday
Francoise	MINOU. Scribner
Gag	MILLIONS OF CATS. Coward-McCann
Henderson	CATS FOR KANSAS. Abingdon
Newberry	APRIL'S KITTENS. Harper
	BABETTE. Harper
	THE KITTENS ABC. Harper
	MARSHMALLOW. Harper
	MITTENS. Harper
	SMUDGE. Harper
Potter	THE TALE OF TIM KITTEN. Warne
Thayer	THE OUTSIDE CAT. Morrow
Will	RUSSET AND THE TWO REDS. Harcourt
	THE TWO REDS. Harcourt
Williams	TIMID TIMOTHY. Scott
Yashima	MOMO'S KITTEN. Viking
Ylla	I'LL SHOW YOU CATS. Harper

Easy-to-Read Books:

Dolch	I LIKE CATS. Garrard
Hurd	COME AND HAVE FUN. Harper
	NO FUNNY BUSINESS. Harper
Minarik	CAT AND DOG. Harper
Vacheron	MORE ABOUT HENRI. Scribner
Seuss	THE CAT IN THE HAT. Random
	THE CAT IN THE HAT COMES BACK. Random

Reference:	Biographical material on Wanda Gag (GAHG)
Gag, Wanda	GROWING PAINS; diaries and drawings for the years 1908-1917. New York, Coward-McCann, 1940. 479 pp.
Horn Book mag.	WANDA GAG ISSUE. Boston, Horn Book, 1947: 157-205.
Kunitz, Stanley J.	THE JUNIOR BOOK OF AUTHORS (2d ed. rev.), edited by Stanley J. Kunitz and Howard Haycraft. New York, Wilson, 1951: 134-135.
Scott, Alma	WANDA GAG, THE STORY OF AN ARTIST. Minneapolis, University of Minnesota Press, 1949. 235 pp.

Filmstrip:

MILLIONS OF CATS. Weston Woods Studio.

The Class Session:

"Many people have written stories about cats and many artists have drawn pictures for stories about cats. Here are some from our own library."

Call attention to a number of books on display.

"One of the most famous of all the cat stories is MILLIONS OF CATS, by Wanda Gag. This is one of the stories that children begged Wanda Gag to tell again and again. Wanda Gag came from a family who loved stories and drawing and painting and music. Every evening the Gag home was filled with music and art. Everyone in the family could paint and draw. When Wanda Gag made her story, MILLIONS OF CATS, into a book for all boys and girls to enjoy, her brother printed the words."

Use either the book or the filmstrip.

After going through the filmstrip reading the story, go through the strip enjoying the illustrations.

Encourage the children to compare illustrations from the books displayed.

Follow-up:

Send the collection of cat stories to the classroom where the children can browse through them and their teacher can select some to read to the class.

The class may write a cat story and each child may make his own illustrations for the story. The children should be guided to appreciate the variety in their own illustrations.

Similar lessons may be developed on the following topics:

BEARS:

Books to Read to Children:

Anglund	COWBOY AND HIS FRIEND. Harcourt
Bright	ME AND THE BEARS. Doubleday
Dalgliesh	THE BEARS ON HEMLOCK MOUNTAIN. Scribner
Fatio	THE HAPPY LION AND THE BEAR. McGraw
Janice	BEAR'S SUNDAY BREAKFAST. Lothrop
	LITTLE BEAR'S CHRISTMAS. Lothrop

McCloskey	BLUEBERRIES FOR SAL. Viking
Brooke	THE STORY OF THE THREE BEARS. Warne
Ward	THE BIGGEST BEAR. Houghton
Ylla	POLAR BEAR BROTHERS. Harper
	TWO LITTLE BEARS. Harper

Easy-to-Read Books:

Berenstein	THE BIG HONEY HUNT. Beginner Books
	THE BIKE LESSON. Beginner Books
Hoff	GRIZZWOLD. Harper
Minarik	FATHER BEAR COMES HOME. Harper
	LITTLE BEAR. Harper
	LITTLE BEAR'S FRIEND. Harper
	LITTLE BEAR'S VISIT. Harper
Sharp	WHERE IS CUBBY BEAR? Steck
	WHO ARE YOU? Steck

Filmstrip:

THE BIGGEST BEAR. Weston Woods Studio
Add poetry about bears to this lesson. Consult anthologies.

MICE:

Books to Read to Children:

Ivimey	COMPLETE VERSION OF YE THREE BLIND MICE. Warne
Brown, P.	CHEERFUL. Harper
Daugherty	THE PICNIC. Viking
Flack	WALTER, THE LAZY MOUSE. Doubleday
Freeman, D.	NORMAN THE DOORMAN. Viking
Freeman, L.	PET OF THE MET. Viking
Gag	SNIPPY AND SNAPPY. Coward-McCann
Potter	THE TALE OF JOHNNY TOWN-MOUSE. Warne
	THE TALE OF MRS. TITTLEMOUSE. Warne
	THE TALE OF TWO BAD MICE. Warne
Titus	ANATOLE. McGraw
	ANATOLE AND THE CAT. McGraw
	ANATOLE AND THE POODLE. McGraw
	ANATOLE OVER PARIS. McGraw
Zion	THE SUGAR MOUSE CAKE. Scribner

Easy-to-Read Books:

Hurd	COME AND HAVE FUN. Harper

Filmstrip:

THREE BLIND MICE. Weston Woods Studio

Add poetry about mice to this lesson. Consult anthologies.

FIRST GRADERS VISIT MIKE'S HOUSE

Purpose:

An introduction to the library and to books by Virginia Lee Burton.

Materials Needed:

Books:

MIKE'S HOUSE, by Julia L. Sauer. Viking
Books by Virginia Lee Burton, published by Houghton.
CHOO CHOO
KATY AND THE BIG SNOW
THE LITTLE HOUSE
MAYBELLE, THE CABLE CAR
MIKE MULLIGAN AND HIS STEAM SHOVEL

Reference Book:

THE JUNIOR BOOK OF AUTHORS, edited by Stanley J. Kunitz and Howard Haycraft. Wilson. p. 62.

Filmstrip:

MIKE MULLIGAN AND HIS STEAM SHOVEL. Weston Woods

The Class Session:

Read or tell: MIKE'S HOUSE. The story of a boy who called the library Mike's House because there is where Mike Mulligan and His Steam Shovel, Mary Ann, can be found. Every time the boy goes to the library he checks out the same book—MIKE MULLIGAN AND HIS STEAM SHOVEL! It is his favorite book and the only one he will check out of the library.

"Mike Mulligan is a favorite with many boys and girls. The story was written by a mother. Her name is Mrs. Demetrios, but when she writes books she uses the name, Virginia Lee Burton. Virginia Lee Burton wrote this book for her son Mike." (Look for the dedication in the book.)

"When Virginia Lee Burton is planning a book, she makes the pictures first. Then she lines all the pictures up in order on the walls of her studio and thinks up the story to go with the pictures."

Show the filmstrip: MIKE MULLIGAN AND HIS STEAM SHOVEL. Discuss favorite parts with the children. Go through the filmstrip the second time without reading the text but just enjoying the illustrations.

Present other books by Virginia Lee Burton:

CHOO CHOO: The Story of a Little Engine Who Ran Away is a story you will enjoy and you will learn something about trains when you read it.

KATY AND THE BIG SNOW is an exciting story that tells about the important work the bulldozers and truck plows have to do when a big snow comes and everyone and everything is "snowed in."

THE LITTLE HOUSE is the story of Virginia Lee Burton's own house that was moved back from the street into a field of daisies with apple trees. This book won the Caldecott Award for the best picture book the year it was published.

MAYBELLE, THE CABLE CAR is a story of San Francisco, California. Virginia Lee Burton remembered the little cable cars that she used to ride when she lived in this city and went to school there when she planned this book.

Follow-up:

Allow the children time to examine the books individually by placing them on a reading table in the classroom.

Discuss the stories and illustrations.

How does Virginia Lee Burton make Mary Ann, Maybelle, Katy and the Little House seem almost like people?

Look for their faces.

Read aloud parts that convey the inner thoughts of these book characters.

What story by Virginia Lee Burton is your favorite?
Tell the part that you liked best.

A LETTER THAT BECAME A BOOK

Purpose:

To present the author Beatrix Potter as a person who was once a little girl.

Materials Needed:

Filmstrip:

THE TALE OF PETER RABBIT. Weston Woods

Books by Beatrix Potter published by Warne.

THE PIE AND THE PATTY PAN
THE STORY OF MISS MOPPET
THE TAILOR OF GLOUCESTER
THE TALE OF BENJAMIN BUNNY
THE TALE OF JEMIMA PUDDLE-DUCK
THE TALE OF JOHNNY TOWN-MOUSE
THE TALE OF MRS. TITTLEMOUSE
THE TALE OF PETER RABBIT
THE TALE OF SQUIRREL NUTKIN
THE TALE OF THE FLOPSY BUNNIES
THE TALE OF TOM KITTEN
THE TALE OF TWO BAD MICE

Reference: Biographical material on Beatrix Potter:

Books:

Crouch, Marcus. BEATRIX POTTER. New York, Walck, 1961.

Kunitz, Stanley J. THE JUNIOR BOOK OF AUTHORS (2d ed. rev.), edited by Stanley J. Kunitz and Howard Haycraft. New York, Wilson, 1951: 247-249.

Lane, Margaret. THE TALE OF BEATRIX POTTER, A Biography. London and New York, F. Warne, 1946. 175 pp.

Potter, Beatrix. THE ART OF BEATRIX POTTER, with an appreciation by Anne Carroll Moore (2d ed.), London and New York, F. Warne, 1956. 336 pp.

Magazines:

Linder, Leslie. "The Art of Beatrix Potter and How It Came to Be," Horn book magazine, v. 31, Oct. 1955: 338-356.

Linder, Leslie. "Beatrix Potter's Code Writing," Horn book magazine, v. 39, Apr. 1963: 141-155.

Miller, Bertha M. "Beatrix Potter and Her Nursery Classics," Horn book magazine, v. 20, May 1944: 214-224.

Potter, Beatrix. "Roots of the Peter Rabbit Tales," Horn book magazine, v. 5, May 1929: 69-72.

The Class Session:

"A long time ago, in the country called England there lived a little girl named Beatrix Potter. Her family was wealthy. They had a lot of money and they owned a lot of land. They owned many farms and many people worked for them. But Beatrix Potter was a lonely little girl. She had a brother, but he was sent away to school. He lived at the school. A teacher came to the Potter home to teach Beatrix. Her parents were very busy. Beatrix had many grownup friends, but no children her own age to play with her. Her parents allowed her to have many pets and she kept some of them in the house. Their house was a very, very large house.

"Beatrix loved pets and she loved to draw and paint. Very often she would draw pictures of her pets. She would draw scenes from inside the house—the dining room, the kitchen, the pantry where food was kept, bedrooms, and all parts of the house. She often made sketches or little drawings of the inside of homes of her friends. She made drawings and paintings of plants and gardens—both flower gardens and vegetable gardens.

"When she was grown up, she had many friends among boys and girls. When she wrote to them she would write storylike letters telling them news about her pets and she would draw pictures in her letters. One of these letters to a little friend who was sick was later made into a book we know as THE TALE OF PETER RABBIT.

"When Beatrix Potter began to write books for boys and girls many people were surprised to find the little animal book characters living in their houses or hiding in their gardens. Beatrix Potter used many of the drawings she had made of homes and gardens of friends in her books. Many of the scenes in her books are paintings of her own home.

"I have the story of Peter Rabbit on a filmstrip which we will enjoy sharing together today. I will read the story and show the pictures and then I will show the pictures and we will talk about them"

Enjoy the illustrations with the class.

Follow-up:

Allow the children to take the entire collection of Beatrix Potter books back to the classroom where they may be placed on their reading table and all may enjoy the illustrations. The classroom teacher may wish to read the stories to the class.

JUST IMAGINE

Purpose:

It is not uncommon for children this age to tell "tales." This lesson is planned to point out to children that imagination is an acceptable activity as opposed to telling a lie.

Materials Needed:

Books in which the imaginative activity is clearly portrayed by a return to the commonplace.

Suggested Books:

Anglund	THE COWBOY AND HIS FRIEND. Harcourt
Bright	ME AND THE BEARS. Doubleday
Bonsall	TELL ME SOME MORE. Harper
Craig	THE DRAGON IN THE CLOCK BOX. Norton
Ets	IN THE FOREST. Viking
Johnson	HAROLD AND THE PURPLE CRAYON. Harper
McClintock	WHAT HAVE I GOT? Harper
Ness	SAM, BANGS AND MOONSHINE. Holt
Ressner	AUGUST EXPLAINS. Harper
Sendak	WHERE THE WILD THINGS ARE. Harper
Seuss	AND TO THINK THAT I SAW IT ON MULBERRY STREET. Random
	THE CAT IN THE HAT. Random
	THE CAT IN THE HAT COMES BACK. Random
	IF I RAN THE CIRCUS. Random
	IF I RAN THE ZOO. Random
	McELLIGOT'S POOL. Random
Slobodkin	CLEAR THE TRACK. Macmillan
	MAGIC MICHAEL. Macmillan
Stolz	EMMETT'S PIG. Harper

The Class Session:

This is a lesson that may be requested by a first grade teacher or it may be recommended to a first grade teacher by the librarian. It is most effective when it meets an immediate need.

"Let's have some fun using our heads! Everyone shut your eyes. Make an elephant come into your head.

"Make your elephant sit down.

"Is your elephant sitting on a chair?

"Is he sitting on the floor? On the ground? In a swing?

"Can you make your elephant sit on a bicycle? That is a very difficult thing for an elephant to do.

"Do you have trouble making your elephant do this?

"What color is your elephant? Is he a big elephant, or a baby elephant?

"Now all eyes open! Wasn't that fun? You have been using your imagination."

Read the book and show the pictures—AUGUST EXPLAINS in which a little bear imagines what it is like to be a boy.

"I have selected some books from our library in which the authors and artists have had fun writing stories and making pictures about boys and girls using their imagination."

Tell something about each book:

MAGIC MICHAEL. Michael has a wonderful imagination. In this book Michael uses his imagination so much that he gets into a lot of trouble. He imagines himself to be a dog, a book, a mop, a stork!

CLEAR THE TRACK. In this book the same Michael imagines his tricycle is a train and he is the engineer—the conductor—the brakeman—everything! How would you like to have him for a little brother?

COWBOY AND HIS FRIEND. In this book a boy imagines he has a bear for a friend. Notice how the author, who also made the pictures for the story, shows the make-believe part.

WHERE THE WILD THINGS ARE. This book tells the story of a boy who was sent to bed without his supper for being wild. He imagines going to a place where terribly wild things are.

AND TO THINK THAT I SAW IT ON MULBERRY STREET. Dr. Seuss probably has one of the most wonderful imaginations of all. In this story, Marco is told to keep his eyes open on the way home from school and to report all that he sees to his father. Everything he sees is so common and ordinary that Marco begins to use his imagination just a little at first and then more and more until his walk home becomes wonderful and exciting. But what will he tell his dad? What do you think his dad will say if Marco tells him about all the things he saw on Mulberry Street? (That he is telling a lie!) Did Marco see these things? (Yes, in his head—in his imagination.)

IF I RAN THE CIRCUS. Dr. Seuss has a wonderful time imagining a circus in the empty lot behind Mr. Sneelock's store. Of course, if he uses Mr. Sneelock's lot he has to give him an important part in the circus. It is fun to imagine Mr. Sneelock doing daring things in the circus. Does he look like the brave kind of person who would dare to do these dangerous tricks?

IF I RAN THE ZOO. This story tells what Gerald McGrew would do if he were the owner of the zoo.

It is fun and exciting to imagine things. It is fun to do it just before you go to sleep at night. If you do it after you are asleep what is it called? (Dreaming.)

Follow-up:

Read a fairy tale with no pictures. Let the children imagine how everything is. Have them illustrate the story.

I CAN READ IT MYSELF

Purpose:

To introduce children to books with controlled vocabulary that they can read.

Materials Needed:

A collection of easy-to-read books.

Filmstrip:

PETUNIA. Weston Woods Studio

The Class Session:

Begin this class session by showing the filmstrip, PETUNIA. Petunia is a goose who convinces herself and everyone around her that she is wise because she possesses a book. A humorous-tragic situation brought about through Petunia's "wise" advice clearly points up the importance of knowing how to read. The story is from the book, PETUNIA, by Roger Duvoisin, published by Knopf.

Follow the showing of the filmstrip with a discussion of Petunia's wisdom. This should lead to the conclusion that owning a book does not make a person wise. One important way of gaining wisdom is learning to read what is printed in books.

"You will find many books on display on the tables today. I would like to have you select one you can read to check out this week. It is wise to choose a book that is not too hard, one that you will have fun reading."

To stimulate interest, point out several, telling just enough about the story or the characters to encourage browsing.

Follow-up:

Reporting on books read. Exchanging of books among class members. Sharing a book by reading a favorite part aloud.

Easy-to-Read Books:

Averill	THE FIRE CAT. Harper
Baker, B.	LITTLE RUNNER OF THE LONGHOUSE. Harper
Bonsall	THE CASE OF THE CAT'S MEOW. Harper
	THE CASE OF THE HUNGRY STRANGER. Harper
	TELL ME SOME MORE. Harper
	WHAT SPOT? Harper
	WHO'S A PEST? Harper
Collier	I KNOW A FARM. Scott
Eastmen	ARE YOU MY MOTHER? Beginner Books
	GO, DOG, GO! Beginner Books
	SAM AND THE FIREFLY. Beginner Books
Friskey	INDIAN TWO FEET AND HIS HORSE. Childrens Press
	MYSTERY OF THE BROKEN BRIDGE. Childrens Press
Guilfoile	NOBODY LISTENS TO ANDREW. Follett

Heilbroner	THE HAPPY BIRTHDAY PRESENT. Harper
	ROBERT, THE ROSE HORSE. Harper
Hoban	TOM AND THE TWO HANDLES. Harper
Hoff	DANNY AND THE DINOSAUR. Harper
	JULIUS. Harper
	LITTLE CHIEF. Harper
	OLIVER. Harper
	SAMMY, THE SEAL. Harper
	STANLEY. Harper
	WHO WILL BE MY FRIEND? Harper
Holland	A BIG BALL OF STRING. Beginner Books
Hurd	COME AND HAVE FUN. Harper
	HURRAY, HURRY. Harper
	LAST ONE HOME IS A GREEN PIG. Harper
	NO FUNNY BUSINESS. Harper
Johnson, C.	A PICTURE FOR HAROLD'S ROOM. Harper
King	MABLE THE WHALE. Follett
La Rue	TINY TOOSEY'S BIRTHDAY. Houghton
	TINY'S BIG UMBRELLA. Houghton
McClintock	A FLY WENT BY. Beginner Books
	WHAT HAVE I GOT? Harper
Minarik	CAT AND DOG. Harper
	FATHER BEAR COMES HOME. Harper
	LITTLE BEAR. Harper
	LITTLE BEAR'S FRIEND. Harper
	LITTLE BEAR'S VISIT. Harper
	NO FIGHTING, NO BITING! Harper
Myrick	THE SECRET THREE. Harper
Rey	CURIOUS GEORGE FLIES A KITE. Houghton
Selsam	LET'S GET TURTLES. Harper
Seuss	THE CAT IN THE HAT. Random
	THE CAT IN THE HAT COMES BACK! Random
	DR. SEUSS' ABC. Beginner Books
Stolz	EMMETT'S PIG. Harper
Tensen	COME TO SEE THE CLOWNS. Reilly & Lee
	COME TO THE CITY. Reilly & Lee
	COME TO THE PET SHOP. Reilly & Lee
	COME TO THE ZOO. Reilly & Lee
Zion	HARRY AND THE LADY NEXT DOOR. Harper

SECOND GRADE

The second grade child is now familiar with library procedures, well-acquainted with the picture book section and secure in his relationship with the librarian. His independent use of the library is encouraged throughout this year. Some second grade children will be exploring the fiction section where books such as those by Carolyn Haywood may be used as an introduction to more difficult books.

Children at this age should be encouraged to read many books through the keeping of attractive gamelike reading records.

The librarian will keep the second grade teacher informed of library material on the second grade reading level that may be used during social studies and science units in the classroom.

Readers this age have enough common background in children's literature that they may engage in lively book discussions stimulated by comparing books that are similar in content or the same story illustrated by several illustrators. They are beginning to develop "taste."

LIBRARY CITIZENSHIP

Purpose:

To emphasize the importance of book care.

Materials Needed:

To recall books with which children have had an earlier acquaintance.

Bookmarks to be duplicated.

MOTHER GOOSE SAYS:

1. Have clean hands before you look at books.
2. Turn our pages carefully.
3. Carry us home and back in plastic bags.
4. Have a safe place to keep us at your home.
5. Bring us back on time.
6. Report any damaged book to your teacher or librarian.
7. DON'T try to mend books at home.
8. Put us on the book truck carefully.
9. Use this bookmark to keep your place.

A letter from a library friend such as the one printed below.

A bulletin board display of book jackets from the following books: **Curious George, The Biggest Bear, Anatole, The Story About Ping, Petunia, Mother Goose, Mop Top, The Three Happy Lions, Bedtime for Frances, The Story of Little Black Sambo.**

The Class Session:

"I have a letter to share with you today from one of your very first book friends. Whom do you think this might be? (Listen to their suggestions which will usually bring out Mother Goose.) She is writing for some of your other friends, too."

Call attention to the bulletin board and spend a little time getting reacquainted with these well-known characters.

"Let's see what she has to say to us."

Dear Boys and Girls,

All your old friends in the library are so happy to see you back for another year of good reading, and we'd like to welcome all the newcomers, too. We hope to get to know you better soon.

During the summer, while you were having your vacation, we had a chance to hold some meetings. We decided that there were a few improvements we'd like you to help us make.

Curious George says he gets so tired being laid face down. He has back trouble. He wants you to use the bookmarks we made for you so you can keep your place the right way.

The Biggest Bear was pretty growly about having his pages torn. He says that he knows you good readers will remember to turn pages from the upper right-hand corner.

Petunia reported that she was dropped in the mud with no plastic bag to protect her. Oh, was she sick!

And poor little Anatole was left to shiver in a snowdrift for three days. You can imagine that he won't be back with us this year.

Remember Ping, the little duck, and how he always got spanked for being late? Well, a little girl kept him out for four whole weeks and finally, after three notes from the librarian, she brought him back. He felt bad all summer, but really he wasn't to blame this time.

Even the Happy Lions complained. They said you didn't put them back on the book truck carefully, and sometimes they slid off on the floor and got their pages all scrunched on the corners.

Mop Top said he'd certainly be happier if everybody that visited with him had clean hands. Now that he has his hair cut he's beginning to see how pleasant it is to be clean and look nice.

And did you know that Little Black Sambo said he wasn't nearly so afraid of those tigers as he was of your little brothers and sisters with their pens, pencils and scissors? He says please, oh please put him in a safe place when he comes to visit at your house.

Oh, but the saddest of all was Frances! Somebody had tried to mend her at home, and what troubles she was having. They used the wrong kind of tape and she was turning all yellow and crinkly. Poor Frances—she groaned and moaned. She said, "Be sure and tell them to report to their teachers any damage and let the book doctors take over. Boys and girls wouldn't want their broken arms and cut fingers fixed up by just anybody either."

All your friends said they knew you'd try to help us. Just remember the suggestions on Old Mother Goose's bookmark.

Happy reading to you all,

Mother Goose and Friends from A to Z

Follow-up Activities:

Encourage the making of Book Care posters to illustrate what each character reminded them to do.

Have children dramatize book characters holding a meeting about their complaints on how they have been treated.

Give special recognition to those children who do report damage that has been caused while the book is in their possession.

MEET CAROLYN HAYWOOD, YOUR HOLIDAY HELPER

Purpose:

To introduce the books of Carolyn Haywood.

To show children that books have holiday chapters that they will enjoy.

To call attention to the location of the fiction section.

To compare the call numbers on easy fiction and the regular fiction books.

Materials Needed:

Author material collected from Harcourt, Brace and World, Inc., 757 3rd Avenue, New York, N. Y. 10017 and William Morrow and Company, Inc., 425 Park Avenue South, New York, N. Y. 10016.

A collection of the Haywood books that are available in your library.

A bulletin board display of Haywood book jackets with letters and pictures you have obtained from the publishers.

The Class Session:

"On our bulletin board today we have some information about a very busy lady. She is both an author and an illustrator of children's books. What does this mean? (She writes and makes the pictures for books.) Do you know the names of any other people who do both of these things?" (They may name Robert McClosky, the Haders, Lois Lenski, Marjorie Flack, Emma Brock, Wanda Gag, C. W. Anderson, Wesley Dennis, Louis Slobodkin.) "What page in a book tells you who the author and illustrator are?" (Title page.)

Show them several title pages on which the author and illustrator are the same and several where the work is done by two individuals.

"Carolyn Haywood has written and illustrated more than twenty books for boys and girls. You'll enjoy them all, for her characters are so much like your friends in the second grade. They have parties and picnics, surprises and secrets; they quarrel with their friends and make up. Sometimes sad things happen to them just as they do to you. One especially pleasant feature of Carolyn Haywood's books is that so many of them have holiday chapters. Many times you ask for holiday books. Now you'll know an additional place to look."

Show them how to locate the holiday chapters in the table of contents.

Select a chapter from one of the following to give them a taste of the Haywood books that have holiday chapters.

CHRISTMAS

Betsy's Little Star, "The Santa Claus Parade." pp. 120-133; "The Present That Had No Shape." pp. 134-148.

Penny and Peter, "Now It Is Christmas." pp. 139-160.

Eddie and the Fire Engine. pp. 94-129.

Eddie's Christmas Card, "How Santa Delivered."

Betsy and the Boys, "The Christmas Fairies." pp. 124-141.

Betsy's Winterhouse, "Christmas Carols and The Birthday Tree." pp. 33-52.

Betsy and Billy, "The Present That Betsy Wanted." pp. 62-77. "Christmas Star." pp. 78-91.

Back to School With Betsy, "The Christmas Sleigh Ride." pp. 124-139. "Father's Funny Dream." pp. 107-123.

HALLOWEEN

Betsy and Billy, "The Halloween Party." pp. 30-44.

Betsy's Little Star, "Billy's Halloween Party." pp. 58-73.

Here Comes the Bus, "The Pumpkin People." pp. 100-120.

EASTER

Back to School With Betsy, "The Easter Chick." pp. 156-176.

VALENTINE'S DAY

Betsy and Billy, "Valentine Hearts." pp. 92-107.

Betsy and the Boys, "Betsy and Her Valentines." pp. 142-155. "A Strange Valentine." pp. 156-175.

MAY DAY

Betsy and Billy, "May Day and Mother Goose." pp. 123-141.

Betsy's Winterhouse, "May Baskets." pp. 169-192.

APRIL FOOLS

Betsy's Winterhouse, "April Fool for Whom?" pp. 148-168.

BIRTHDAYS

Betsy's Winterhouse, "Christmas Carols and the Birthday Tree." pp. 33-52.

Here Comes the Bus, "The Forgotten Cake." pp. 68-83. "Who's Got the Cake?" pp. 84-99.

"Carolyn Haywood's books are in the part of our library that we call the FICTION section. Just as in the EASY section where we have been finding many of our books, these fiction books are arranged in alphabetical order according to the author's last name. For what letter will we look to find Carolyn Haywood's books?" (H, or Ha.)

Have them locate several Haywood books in the FICTION section.

Follow-up Activities:

Write and illustrate a chapter of your own for a Carolyn Haywood booklet.

Dramatize your favorite chapter from a Haywood book.

Make a collection of pictures to represent favorite Haywood characters.

AN ILLUSTRATOR MAKES THE PICTURES

Purpose:

To help the child grow in appreciation of the fine art work and the artists responsible for the lovely illustrations in picture books for boys and girls.

Materials Needed:

A collection of books written and illustrated by an outstanding illustrator of books for children.

Leo Politi, author and illustrator of:

ALL THINGS BRIGHT AND BEAUTIFUL. Scribners
A BOAT FOR PEPPE. Scribners
THE BUTTERFLIES COME. Scribners
JUANITA. Scribners
LITO AND THE CLOWN. Scribners
LITTLE LEO. Scribners
THE MISSION BELL. Scribners
MOY MOY. Scribners
PEDRO THE ANGEL OF OLVERA STREET. Scribners
SAINT FRANCIS AND THE ANIMALS. Scribners
SONG OF THE SWALLOWS. Scribners
ROSA. Scribners

Biographical material and pictures from the Charles Scribner's Sons, Publishers. 597 5th Ave., New York, N. Y. 10017.

Book jackets for bulletin board display.

A map of California, a map of the United States and a globe.

Reference:

Kunitz, Stanley J. THE JUNIOR BOOK OF AUTHORS (2d ed. rev.), edited by Stanley J. Kunitz and Howard Haycraft. New York, Wilson, 1951. p. 247

The Class Session:

Have a bulletin board display of pictures of Leo Politi and book jackets from several of his books.

"Leo Politi lives in Los Angeles, California. He was born in Fresno, California. When Leo was seven years old, the family decided to return to his parents' old home in Italy. The Indian costume Leo had brought with him from America caused so much interest and excitement that the teacher had to ask his mother not to let him wear it to school. This is the way Leo Politi tells this story in the book LITTLE LEO."

Tell the story, LITTLE LEO, using the illustrations in the book.
Use the globe to point out the travels of the Politi family from California to New York and across the Atlantic Ocean to Italy.

"When Leo Politi finished high school in Italy, he returned to the United States and moved to California where he now lives."

Locate the United States on the globe. Display a map of the United States, pointing out California in relationship to your own state. Using a map of the state of California, point out the locale of the following books:

SONG OF THE SWALLOWS—Capistrano
LITTLE LEO—Fresno
THE BUTTERFLIES COME—Monterey
MOY MOY—Chanking Street in Los Angeles
JUANITA—Olvera Street in old Los Angeles

Examine the illustrations in books written and illustrated by Leo Politi. Notice his happy, round-faced children. Point out that the scenes are true pictures of places in California and near his home in Los Angeles.

Follow-up Activities:

Autumn is a good time to read the story of the monarch butterfly, THE BUTTERFLIES COME. This story tells of the migration of monarch butterflies to Monterey and the celebration of their arrival.

Use the book ROSA to introduce books by Leo Politi during the Christmas season, or use JUANITA if introducing his books near Easter.

Spring is a good time to use the book SONG OF THE SWALLOWS when children are waiting for the return of the birds.

Similar lessons may be developed introducing the work of author-artists who write about everyday happenings in their immediate environment or about places very familiar to them.

Bemelmans, Ludwig
MADELINE. Viking (Paris, France)
MADELINE AND THE BAD HAT. Viking (Paris, France)
MADELINE AND THE GYPSIES. Viking (Chartres, Deauville, and Avignon in France)
MADELINE IN LONDON. Viking (London, England)
MADELINE'S RESCUE. Viking (Paris, France)

McCloskey, Robert
Stories and pictures with the family summer home off the coast of Maine as the setting, and characters patterned after his own family:
BLUEBERRIES FOR SAL. Viking
ONE MORNING IN MAINE. Viking
TIME OF WONDER. Viking

A LION IS ROAR AND MORE

Purpose:

To enjoy a variety of illustrations depicting lions.

To appreciate the fact that everyone does not see things in the same way.

To present some of the best in children's literature for appreciation and enjoyment.

To stimulate an awareness of art in children's books.

Materials Needed:

Books with illustrations of lions. Suggested titles:

THE SLEEPY LITTLE LION. Brown, M. W., photo by Ylla. Harper.
ANDY AND THE LION. Daugherty. Viking.
THE PICNIC. Daugherty. Viking.
LION. DuBois. Viking.
THE HAPPY LION. Fatio. Viking. Pictures by R. Duvoisin.
THE HAPPY LION AND THE BEAR. Fatio. Viking. Pictures by R. Duvoisin.
THE HAPPY LION IN AFRICA. Fatio. Viking. Pictures by R. Duvoisin.
THE HAPPY LION ROARS. Fatio. Viking. Pictures by R. Duvoisin.
THE HAPPY LION'S QUEST. Fatio. Viking. Pictures by R. Duvoisin.
THREE HAPPY LIONS. Fatio. Viking. Pictures by R. Duvoisin.
THE LION AND THE RAT. LaFontaine. Watts. Pictures by Brian Wildsmith.
HUBERT'S HAIR-RAISING ADVENTURE. Peet.
RANDY'S DANDY LIONS. Peet.
IF I RAN THE ZOO. Seuss. Random.

The Class Session:

Read to the class the story, **Lion, by** William Pene DuBois. This is the story of the creation of the very first lion. Enjoy the story and the illustrations.

"Many different artists have portrayed the lion. Here are some books from our library in which lions are pictured."

Photographs by Ylla.

The muscular lions by James Daugherty in ANDY AND THE LION and THE PICNIC.

The fierce yet friendly lion in THE HAPPY LION books illustrated by Roger Duvoisin.

The colorful lion pictures by Brian Wildsmith in THE LION AND THE RAT.

The scraggly comic lions drawn by Bill Peet in HUBERT'S HAIR-RAISING ADVENTURE and RANDY'S DANDY LION.

The impossible lion from McGrew's Zoo in Dr. Seuss' IF I RAN THE ZOO.

"Notice that in the colored illustrations the artists are true to the tawny color of the lion as we like to think of him."

"Which artist's lions do you like the best? Why?"

"Why do you suppose the lion has been called the 'King of Beasts'?"

"Which lion would you be most afraid to meet on a path in the woods or jungle?"

"Which lion would you like to meet on a path in the woods?"

Follow-up Activities:

Enjoy each of the stories at a later date.

Display in the classroom paintings by famous artists in which lions are portrayed.

Have each child make a drawing of a lion as he thinks it should look. Encourage originality.

Variation: Look at trees.

Suggested Books:

Bemelmans. PARSLEY. Harper.

Birnbaum. GREEN EYES. Capitol Pub.

Burton. THE LITTLE HOUSE. Houghton.

Ets. GILBERTO AND THE WIND. Viking.

Hader. THE BIG SNOW. Macmillan.

Keats. THE SNOWY DAY. Viking.

Langstaff. FROG WENT A-COURTIN'. Harcourt. Illustrations by F. Rojankovsky.

Leaf. THE STORY OF FERDINAND. Viking. Illustrations by R. Lawson.

McCloskey. TIME OF WONDER. Viking.

MacDonald. THE LITTLE ISLAND. Doubleday. Illustrations by L. Weisgard.

Scheer. RAIN MAKES APPLESAUCE. Holiday. Illustrations by M. Bileck.

Seuss. HORTON HATCHES THE EGG. Random.

Slobodkin. WIDE-AWAKE OWL.

Tresselt. JOHNNY MAPLE-LEAF. Illustrations by R. Duvoisin.

Udry. A TREE IS NICE. Harper. Illustrations by M. Simont.

Ward. THE BIGGEST BEAR. Houghton.

Introduce this study of trees through the reading of A TREE IS NIC

Suitable subjects that may be used in a similar manner:
    Cats, Mice, Monkeys, Dogs, Cows, Horses.

BOYS AND GIRLS VISIT MR. PUMPKIN'S FARM

Purpose:

To introduce the books of the well-known artist Roger Duvoisin with emphasis on the books he has both written and illustrated.

Materials Needed:

Books by Roger Duvoisin:

LONELY VERONICA. Knopf
PETUNIA. Knopf
PETUNIA BEWARE. Knopf
PETUNIA I LOVE YOU. Knopf
VERONICA. Knopf
VERONICA'S SMILE. Knopf

Book jackets, picture, chart with information about Roger Duvoisin for bulletin board display.

Reference:

Biographical material and pictures of Roger Duvoisin from Alfred A. Knopf, Inc. 501 Madison Avenue, New York, N. Y. 10022.
JUNIOR BOOK OF AUTHORS (2nd ed. rev.) edited by Stanley J. Kunitz and Howard Haycraft. New York, Wilson, 1951: 106-107.

The Class Session:

On the bulletin board display a picture of Roger Duvoisin along with jackets from a book about Petunia and a book about Veronica. A chart story on the bulletin board may give a bit of information about the artist-author. See the JUNIOR BOOK OF AUTHORS for remarks Roger Duvoisin makes about the difficulty he has with drawing horses and trees. A question at the end of the chart story such as, "Do you like the pictures of the horse, Straw, in the books about Petunia?" should tease the children's curiosity and lead them to examine the illustrations in the books by Roger Duvoisin.

Call attention to the bulletin board. Tell something of interest about Roger Duvoisin.

"Roger Duvoisin and his wife live in the country with mountains close by. They are very fond of animals and often get ideas for their books about their own animals on their farm. Roger Duvoisin enjoys telling stories to children. He told them to his own children and to his grandchildren, and now boys and girls everywhere can enjoy his stories because they have been made into books and he has made pictures to go with the stories."

"Petunia is a favorite book friend. Let's meet her and the other animals on Mr. Pumpkin's farm."

Show the filmstrip, PETUNIA.

The showing of the filmstrip, PETUNIA, will introduce the children to the animals on Mr. Pumpkin's farm. If this filmstrip has been used at another time, it will be fun to recall what happened to Petunia when she thought she was "wise." (When Petunia found a book, she decided to take it with her, to love it, and become wise in so doing. Through a series of near catastrophies brought about through Petunia's "wise" council, she comes to the realization that—It is not enough to carry wisdom under her wing. She must put it in her mind and in her heart and to do this she must learn to read.)

Identify the main characters:

     Mr. Pumpkin, the farmer
     Bobby, Mr. Pumpkin's grandson
     Petunia, the goose
     Ida, the hen
     Clover, the cow
     Straw, the horse
     Noisy, the dog
     Cotton, the cat
     King, the rooster

"Here are more books about our friend, Petunia, and the other animals on Mr. Pumpkin's farm."

These stories present many opportunities for the children to anticipate what happens next! They are helpful in enriching vocabulary.

PETUNIA BEWARE! "Petunia wanted what she didn't have. She went about looking for greener meadows than her own in spite of her friends' warnings about wild animals she might encounter. When Noisy, the dog, rescues her from Weasel, Fox, Raccoon and Bobcat, Petunia realizes the grass in her own meadow is the best she ever tasted."

I LOVE YOU PETUNIA. "Raccoon flatters Petunia with words of admiration and love. What he would **love** is Petunia for his dinner. When Petunia becomes his friend, when he is in need, they become friends indeed!"

"You must meet another friend from the books by Roger Duvoisin. Here is Veronica!" **(Veronica).**

"What kind of animal is she? (Hippopotamus.) Is Veronica a farm animal? (No.) Where would you have to go to find an animal like Veronica? (Zoo or jungle.)"

"Here we meet Veronica at home with her family and friends in the jungle. Veronica wanted to be different. In fact, she wanted very much to be famous. So she left the river and her many hippopotamus relatives and friends and wandered off to the city where she had many adventures.

Veronica was even arrested and put in jail! She was glad when a kindly lady arranged for her return to her mudbank on the river where she became famous because of her adventures in the city."

"Veronica has another interesting adventure."

Present the book, VERONICA GOES TO PETUNIA'S FARM.

"Veronica liked Mr. Pumpkin's farm as soon as she stepped out of the delivery van. The animals all decide they do not like Veronica because she doesn't look like a farm animal. When the farm animals ignore her, poor Veronica becomes lonely and sad. She loses her appetite and becomes ill. The farm animals become concerned and each one brings food, and to their joy Veronica recovers and becomes a part of the happy farmyard family."

"Veronica has another adventure on Mr. Pumpkin's farm."

Present the book, VERONICA'S SMILE.

"Mr. Pumpkin and all the animals on the farm have work to do. Everyone has important work to do except Veronica. She is bored. Veronica becomes a very important animal on the farm when she discovers that by using her huge mouth she is able to rescue her animal friends from danger. She even rescues Bobby, Mr. Pumpkin's grandson! Petunia notices how happy everyone is when each one does what he can do with what he has."

Follow-up Activities:

Have a collection of books by Roger Duvoisin in the classroom available for browsing and enjoying the illustrations.

Make a mural of Mr. Pumpkin's farm and Veronica's river.

WORKING TOGETHER TO MAKE A BOOK

Berta and Elmer Hader

Purpose:

To interest children in the way in which authors and artists work together to create a picture book.

To introduce Berta and Elmer Hader and their books as an example of the result of cooperative planning and working to create picture books.

Materials Needed:

Biographical Material:

Biographical material and pictures from:

The Macmillan Company, Publishers, 866 3rd Avenue, New York, N. Y. 10019.

THE JUNIOR BOOK OF AUTHORS (2nd ed. rev.), edited by Stanley J. Kunitz and Howard Haycraft. New York, Wilson, 1951: 148-150.

Elementary English magazine. Vol. XXXII, No. 8, December 1955. pp. 501-506.

Books:

THE BIG SNOW
COCK-A-DOODLE-DO
DING DONG BELL
THE FARMER IN THE DELL
THE FRIENDLY PHOEBE
LITTLE APPALOOSA
LITTLE CHIP
THE LITTLE STONE HOUSE
LITTLE WHITE FOOT
LOST IN THE ZOO
THE MIGHTY HUNTER
MR. BILLY'S GUN
PANCHO
THE RUNAWAYS
SQUIRRELY OF WILLOW HILL
TWO IS COMPANY, THREE'S A CROWD
WISH ON THE MOON

Filmstrips:

FS 25 THE BIG SNOW, Weston Woods Studio
FS 23 PANCHO, Weston Woods Studio

The Class Session:

Who are Berta and Elmer Hader?

(Use information from the JUNIOR BOOK OF AUTHORS, the December 1955 issue of the "Elementary English" magazine, and biographical information furnished by the Macmillan Publishing Company.)

Where do they live?

"Berta and Elmer Hader have a most interesting home. They searched until they found just the right spot for building their home, and they built it themselves. They tell the story of their home in this book:

THE LITTLE STONE HOUSE.

In telling the story, they have used the Doe family in place of themselves."

(Tell the story from the book, using the pictures.)

"The Haders get many letters from boys and girls asking them where they get their ideas for books and how they go about making a book. Here is a letter they have written to you answering the questions that boys and girls most often ask."

Dear Girls and Boys:

We live in a stone house which we built ourselves on the west shore of the Tappan Zee. The Tappan Zee is a wide bay in the Hudson River, about thirty miles north of New York City. Our house is on a steep bank, which was once part of a stone quarry. A spring bubbles up under our house and tumbles down the hillside in a series of waterfalls to a small pool at the foot of the hill and over the edge of the pool to a little stream that flows into the mighty Hudson.

We are often asked where we get our ideas for stories. When one thinks about writing a story, or making a picture book, ideas come from every direction. For example, when we were building our house, we found that there was plenty of fun mixed with the hard work. We thought it would be amusing to write a story about building a home, so we wrote "THE LITTLE STONE HOUSE."

Our house is surrounded by trees and bushes and vines in a wild tangle, so there are many birds and little animals living close by. Our adventures with these birds and animals suggested stories to us and we wrote "LITTLE CHIP," the adventures of chipmunks which lived on our hill, and "SQUIRRELY," about a baby squirrel found in our woodland, which grew up in our house, and the "FRIENDLY PHOEBE" is the story of a bird we raised after we found him in a deserted nest.

One winter a very heavy snow covered all the countryside and the birds and squirrels and deer were hungry, so we put out extra helpings of seed for the birds and squirrels and bought hay for the deer. This experience gave us the idea for "THE BIG SNOW." "LOST IN THE ZOO" was suggested to us when we read in the newspaper the story of a little boy who was lost but didn't realize that all the people he saw were looking for him. Another time we read of a kind farmer who fed some wild geese on a pond near his house. The next year more geese came and more and more every year. We thought this would make an interesting book and we wrote "TWO IS COMPANY, THREE'S A CROWD."

So you see, ideas for stories are everywhere. Perhaps you will write storybooks some day. We hope you do, for it is fun to write stories and draw the pictures, too.

With all good wishes,

Berta and Elmer Hader

BERTA AND ELMER HADER

"The book, THE BIG SNOW, that the Haders tell about in their letter to you, won a prize for the best picture book of the year in the year it was published. It is a favorite picture book in our library. In it we see their home and many of the animals that live in the woods that surround the house. We can see the vegetable garden, the river, and best of all, we can see Berta and Elmer working hard to feed the hungry birds and animals whose food has been covered by the big snow."

Use the filmstrip or the book, taking time to enjoy the illustrations.

The children will enjoy comparing a picture of Berta and Elmer Hader with the illustrations they have made of themselves in the book, THE BIG SNOW.

"Berta and Elmer want children to have fun reading their books. They have a special way of including some fun in each of their books."

Open a book to the title page. Read the title page and comment on the illustration.

Encourage children to guess what the story will be about.

"On the back of the title page Berta and Elmer Hader have drawn a funny little picture of themselves. The picture goes along with the theme or setting of the story."

THE BIG SNOW shows Berta and Elmer resting on their shovels after clearing the walks and feeding the animals.

COCK-A-DOODLE-DO shows Berta and Elmer dressed as farmers feeding the chickens.

DING DONG BELL has a picture of Berta and Elmer with the cat, Tiger, and one of the dollar bills the cat found in the old well.

LOST IN THE ZOO has one of the funniest pictures of all. It shows Berta and Elmer in a cage at the zoo!

"I will send all our books by Berta and Elmer Hader to your room so that you may all enjoy looking at the lovely illustrations. You may enjoy playing the guessing game—looking at the title page and trying to guess what Berta and Elmer will look like in the funny little drawing on the back of the title page. Your teacher will want to read many of the stories to your class."

Follow-up Activities:

At a later date, after the children have had a chance to enjoy a number of books by the Haders, you may enjoy a class discussion. Ask, "What do you know about Berta and Elmer Hader?" (They like animals. They like boys and girls. They make up stories and pictures together. Sometimes they write about the animals that live near their home. They built their own home, etc.)

If the children have had the experience of being introduced to several illustrators, a game may be played that will check whether or not they recognize the artists' techniques or styles. Plan to show the work of five illustrators. Open each of the five books selected to an illustration that is typical of the artist's work. Give each illustration a number. If the children wish to indicate illustration No. 1, they hold up one finger, etc. Ask, "Which illustration was made by Leo Politi?" (Children should recognize the little round-faced children.) If this book is numbered 3, the children who recognize Leo Politi's illustration will hold up three fingers in response to the question. Ask, "Can you find the book that has pictures by Berta and Elmer Hader? "Which picture was made by Roger Duvoisin? By Beatrix Potter? By Dr. Seuss?" Someone who has responded correctly may be called upon to tell the class why he thinks the illustration was made by that artist.

(Beatrix Potter—The tiny book has tiny pictures of real animals wearing clothes. Berta and Elmer Hader—The animals look so realistic. Roger Duvoisin—He draws good animals but they don't look furry and real. They are the kind of animals that talk. Dr. Seuss—His illustrations are funny.)

The storyhours for the year may be centered around books by couples who work together. Biographical material and pictures may be secured from their publishers. After enjoying several books created by a couple, the class may wish to write a letter to the author-illustrator team. The letters may be sent to them in care of their publishers.

Ingri and Edgar Parin d'Aulaire
Conrad and Mary Buff
Louise Fatio and Roger Duvoisin
Lillian and Russell Hoban
Maud and Miska Petersham
Ann and Paul Rand
H. A. Rey and Margaret Rey
Herman and Nina Schneider
Florence and Louis Slobodkin
Lynn Ward and May McNeer

THIRD GRADE

Interest in picture books at this level may be extended by presenting Caldecott Award Winning Books.

In the area of fiction books, children may now be guided from Carolyn Haywood's books which are within their own experiences to those books with settings and situations less familiar. Their expanded interest in fiction can be used to provide an introduction to fairy tales and the nonfiction section of the library.

The realization that nonfiction books can be located easily because like subjects are grouped together on the shelves will serve as a motivation for the introduction of biography, science, and poetry.

Interest in authors and illustrators as people who are interested in children as readers brings a sense of satisfaction to the children. Getting to know an author through his books becomes a new adventure.

With expanding interests in topics and new interest in the people responsible for books, the third grade looks to the librarian for help and guidance. A longer library period is needed for this class to explore the "new" areas of the library and to pursue varied interests that require much individual reader guidance.

LIBRARY CITIZENSHIP

Purpose:

To review book care and library conduct.
To reinforce attitudes of responsibility for shared property.
To discuss the proper use of the library by groups and individuals.

Materials Needed:

A tape recording of the book's message (see below).

The Class Session:

"We have talked before on your visits to the library about how we should act while we're here and how we should handle our books. We all know that when we go to the gym we have lots of room to run and play. Why can't we do these things in the library? (The library should be a quiet place where people can enjoy their reading. There are many sharp edges where we could get hurt if we ran or pushed each other.) Would you like to have someone sit down in the middle of the gym floor to read his books? Why not? (It would interfere with our games. He would be in the way.) We are very lucky that our school has special rooms so we can do many activities. Good citizens will observe the rules in each special room so that others may have their fair time to do what they wish."

"To whom do the books in our library belong?"

Help the children see that they belong to the whole group and are paid for by taxes. Encourage them to talk to their parents about taxes and public property.

"Here's a message from a book in your library:"

This could be read by you, or someone the children didn't recognize, and tape recorded. Have a dummy book made up as the speaker.

"Listen to see what this book is worrying about."

A BOOK TALKS TO YOU

I'm a book from your library—I'm old and I'm new
    And I want to be special friends with you.
Will you keep me dry in a plastic bag
    So my pages won't wrinkle nor my edges sag?
Will you use a bookmark to keep your place,
    And never lay me flat on my face?
Will you put me up high so baby dear,
    Won't cut and color or tear and smear?
Will you wash your hands when you handle me,
    So I can keep clean and be pleasing to see?
Will you turn my pages with the greatest of care,
    So they won't be ruined by wrinkle or tear?
Will you bring me back on the date I'm due,
    So overdue slips won't keep coming to you?
Will you report if you do have bad luck,
    And not hide me away on the library truck?

I want to make friends with each girl and boy
    And with you I'll share all kinds of joy.
I tell you of pets, of fairies, of space,
    Of birds, and of lions and of cars that race.
I'll take you off on a flight to the moon,
    And let you taste from my wishing spoon.
I'll catch you a leprechaun just for fun,
    And let you watch how a train is run.
So be my friend—let no one say
    That you weren't good to your book today!

Discuss the book's worries. Encourage honesty in reporting book damage.

"If your book does get torn or crayon-marked or damaged in any way, don't try to fix it at home. The library has special materials to work with and special book doctors to take care of the book's injuries. Let us do the job right."

Distribute bookmarks. Publishing companies are most generous about furnishing supplies of this kind.

Follow-up Activities:

Ditto the book poem and let children decorate it for the library corner in their room.

Encourage them to make book care posters for the library.

Suggest that they make and decorate their own book carrying bags.

Make a display of a group of books that have needed to go to the book hospital.

Make a chart showing the cost of some of the children's favorite books. This information could be used in their math classes.

Have a bookmark contest—the winner to have his bookmark reproduced for all to share.

ILLUSTRATORS

Purpose:

To introduce several books which have been awarded the Caldecott Medal.
To develop an awareness of the illustrator's part in making a book.
To examine how several artists handle the same subject.

Materials Needed:

Filmstrips available from Weston Woods, Weston, Connecticut 06889:

Fs61 **The Snowy Day** by Ezra Keats
Fs25 **The Big Snow** by Berta and Elmer Hader
Fs24 **White Snow, Bright Snow** illustrated by Roger Duvoisin

The Class Session:

"We have talked about the Caldecott Medal that is awarded each year to the picture book chosen for the quality of its illustrations. Today we are going to have a chance to see how three different illustrators handle the same subject. That subject is 'snow.' Berta and Elmer Hader have written the book, **The Big Snow,** for which they have also made the illustrations. As I show you the filmstrip, be thinking how you would describe their illustrations."

After the filmstrip has been shown, discuss reactions. It should be brought out that the Haders' illustrations are realistic and that the ideas expressed are the problems faced by the animal world.

"The next story, **White Snow, Bright Snow**, was written by Alvin Tresselt, but the illustrations were made by Roger Duvoisin. In what way is the subject of 'snow' treated by this book?"

After this filmstrip has been shown, <u>discuss</u> their reactions. Bring out the idea that the theme this time was the effect of snow on community helpers. Help them to see that although Mr. Duvoisin does not attempt to make his pictures realistic, one gets the feeling of what the author is trying to say because of the brilliance of his colors, the humorous things the people are doing.

"The third filmstrip we will examine is called **A Snowy Day.** Both the story and the pictures are by Ezra Keats. In what ways are this book different from the other two?"

As you discuss this filmstrip, help the children to see that Mr. Keats has used a method of illustration called collage in which he combined different kinds of materials such as cloth and various textures of paper to produce the desired effects. The story here is that of a little boy's activities on a snowy day.

"What kind of illustrations did you like best? Why did all three of these books win Caldecott Medals?"

Follow-up Activities:

Compare the sea illustrations for **Time of Wonder** and **The Little Island.**

Decide why the artists for these three picture books made their animals so differently: **The Biggest Bear, Finders Keepers** and **Frog Went A-Courtin'.**

Make a collection of illustrations secured from the publishers. Frequently show a few of them to the class until they become skilled at recognizing some of the well-known artists' techniques.

THE CALDECOTT MEDAL WINNERS

Purpose:

To give children an opportunity to examine and become familiar with the Caldecott Award picture books.

To develop an appreciation for the work of an illustrator.

Materials Needed:

Caldecott Award Bookmarks—available from The Children's Book Council, Inc., 175 Fifth Ave., New York, N. Y. 10010. Cost, 100 for $1.50.

Bulletin board display of Caldecott Award book jackets with Caldecott Medal.

A collection of Caldecott Award-winning books.

The Class Session:

"In almost every book there is a very important page that gives us a great deal of information about the book. What is this page called? (The title page.) What kinds of information does the title page give us? (Title, author, illustrator, publisher, place of publication, copyright date.) What is the work of the illustrator? How do you think an illustrator gets ready to do his work?" (Reads the book and tries to imagine how the characters should look; whether real or imaginary creatures would be better; whether light or dark colors would express the idea of the book; just what kind of art materials [watercolor, line drawings, paper cutting, block printing] would be best to use.)

"Some illustrators become very famous. Can you name some that you remember from your favorite picture books?"

"Every year a picture book is chosen as the best one for that year. The artist or illustrator is awarded the Caldecott Medal for his work. This medal is named after a very famous English illustrator named Randolph Caldecott and has engraved on it a design which he made."

Pass out the Caldecott bookmarks and call attention to the design which is on the medal. Show several book jackets to which the medal has been affixed.

"I have collected the Caldecott Medal winners from our library so that you may have a chance to become better acquainted with them. The collection will be kept in your room for the next month. As you read the books, put a check on the bookmark I have given you. Decide whether you like the way the artist's pictures help to tell the story."

"Two artists have each won the award twice. This is a very special honor. What two artists have had this honor?" (Robert McCloskey's **Time of Wonder** and **Make Way for Ducklings**; Marcia Brown's **Cinderella** and **Once a Mouse.**)

"As you read other books, check the title pages for the illustrator's name. See if you can learn to identify the work of an artist, and then check to see how often you have made the right guess."

"What are some words and phrases we might use to describe the art work of the books we are going to examine?" (Realistic, brilliant colors, funny, imaginative, lively, strange, lots of action, many details, beautiful, dark, mysterious, very different, pale, etc.)

Follow-up Activities:

From discarded Caldecott books collect a series of pictures which can be used to help children identify the style of the various artists. By using 4 or 5 such pictures at a time and displaying other books by the same illustrator, see how many they can match up.

Ask interested children to choose a favorite illustrator and try to copy a picture that best shows his style. Use them for a bulletin board display along with the illustrator's book jacket.

ARRANGEMENT OF FICTION BOOKS

Purpose:

To teach how fiction books can be located by author letter.

To discuss favorite authors.

Materials Needed:

Blackboard or chart paper.

Slips on which are written the titles and authors of books which children will enjoy reading. Below is a suggested list:

HERE COMES KRISTIE by Emma Brock (Knopf)

RIDING THE PONY EXPRESS by Clyde Robert Bulla (Crowell)

THE FAMILY UNDER THE BRIDGE by Natalie Carlson (Harper)

HENRY HUGGINS by Beverly Cleary (Morrow)

THE COURAGE OF SARAH NOBLE by Alice Dalgliesh

TATSINDA by Elizabeth Enright (Harcourt)

THE HUNDRED DRESSES by Eleanor Estes (Harcourt)

THE BIG BLACK HORSE by Walter Farley (Random House)

MELINDY'S MEDAL by Georgene Faulkner (Messner)

MY FATHER'S DRAGON by Ruth Gannett (Random House)

PILGRIM THANKSGIVING by Wilma Hays (Coward-McCann)

"B" IS FOR BETSY by Carolyn Haywood (Harcourt)

TWIG by Elizabeth Jones (Macmillan)

LITTLE PEAR by Eleanor Lattimore (Morrow)

RABBIT HILL by Robert Lawson (Viking)

PIPPI LONGSTOCKING by Astrid Lindgren (Viking)

THE GOLDEN NAME DAY by Jennie Lindquist (Harper)

THE STORY OF DR. DOLITTLE by Hugh Lofting (Lippincott)

BETSY-TACY by Maud Hart Lovelace (Crowell)

A PONY CALLED LIGHTNING by Miriam Mason (Macmillan)

NICKY'S FOOTBALL TEAM by Marion Renick (Scribner)

THE CRICKET IN TIMES SQUARE by George Selden (Farrar, Straus)

SPACE SHIP UNDER THE APPLE TREE by Louis Slobodkin (Macmillan)

BASIL OF BAKER STREET by Eve Titus (McGraw)

SPACE CAT by Ruthven Todd (Scribner)

TAKAO AND GRANDFATHER'S SWORD by Yoshiko Uchida (Scribner)

The Class Session:

"What is the name given to a person who writes a book?" (Author).

"Who is your favorite author? What did he write?"

As the authors are suggested, write their names on the chart or on the blackboard with the titles given beside them. Many of the titles suggested will be EASY books, but these will serve as well to illustrate the object of the lesson.

71

"How do you find a book by your favorite author in our library?"

Give several volunteers a chance to look. Have them explain to the class what they are doing.

Call the children's attention to the list of titles and authors that is on the chart or the blackboard.

"These are your favorites. What clue helps you find your special book friend on the shelf?" (Author's name.)

Give each child a chance to come to the chart and draw a circle around the first two letters of his author's last name.

"Today we're going to play a game called 'FIND A FICTION BOOK.' Each of you will be given a slip of paper on which is written the title of a book and the name of its author. Draw a circle around the first two letters of your author's last name. Show your slip to me. Now you are ready to go to the fiction shelves. Track down the two letters you have circled. Look for the title of the book. When you find it, pull it out to the edge of the shelf and wait beside it until I check your find."

Demonstrate by writing a sample on the board, circling the author letter and finding the book on the shelf.

"If the book you find is one you would like to read, you may check it out after I have collected your finding slip."

Follow-up Activities:

Encourage children to make up riddles which involve the finding of a certain book. Example: I know a book about a nice little old lady who helped bad children turn into better children. The author letters are MA (Mrs. Piggle-Wiggle). Find it on the shelf.

I know a book about a little girl who had supper with George Washington. The author letters are Fr (The Cabin Faced West).

Help children to use the author clues from the book jackets used in bulletin board displays.

MEETING AN AUTHOR

Purpose:

To help children realize that an author is a real person whose background and experiences influence his writing.

To introduce books written by Clyde Robert Bulla.

Materials Needed:

Bookmarks advertising the books written by Clyde Robert Bulla are available from The Crowell-Collier Publishing Company, 640 Fifth Ave., New York, N. Y. 10019.

A bulletin board of book jackets from Mr. Bulla's books.

A collection of Mr. Bulla's books from your library.

The Class Session:

"How many of you have ever met an author?"

Take time to discuss this point, for some of the children have had this experience.

"Today, although our author couldn't be with us in person, he has done the next best thing. He has written us a letter answering questions about himself that he thinks we'd like to ask him. His name is Clyde Robert Bulla."

Dear Boys and Girls,

When I was a boy I lived on a farm in Missouri. My first school was a one-room schoolhouse in the country. Our library was small. At school or at home it seemed I never had enough books to read.

Very early I knew I wanted to be a writer. The first story I started was called HOW PLANETS WERE BORN. I was 7 or 8 at the time.

It was more than ten years later before my stories began to be published. For awhile I wrote magazine stories, then went to work on a newspaper in my home town. During those newspaper years, I wrote THE DONKEY CART, a book for boys and girls. By the time it was published, I was at work on another one—RIDING THE PONY EXPRESS.

I came to California to live and write. Besides writing, one of the things I enjoy most is traveling. I have made trips through the United States, Canada and Mexico, and to most of the countries in Europe. My favorite way to travel is on a freight-boat, especially one that stops at strange, out-of-the-way places.

The question that readers most often ask me is: Where do you get your ideas? Ideas are everywhere—in something you see or hear, in something you read, in something you remember.

When I wrote THE DONKEY CART, A DOG NAMED PENNY, and THREE-DOLLAR MULE, I was remembering life on the farm. One night, in the middle of a Western ghost town, I began to wonder why the town was dark and empty, why everyone had gone away. Out of my wondering came a book—GHOST TOWN TREASURE. In the British Isles I went through an old castle with a group of school children. This gave me the idea for a story about a boy who lived in a castle in long-ago times. The story was THE SWORD IN THE TREE. Once I heard someone talking about the old days in our country when log-rafts were floated down the great rivers. I began to picture the life of a boy on one of the rafts. The book that came out of this was DOWN THE MISSISSIPPI.

73

But a book needs more than an idea. It needs characters and a story. Almost always it needs research. Sometimes the writing takes months.

Altogether I have written thirty-five books for boys and girls. I hope to write many more.

Your friend,
CLYDE ROBERT BULLA

After the letter has been read, discuss with the class reasons why they think Mr. Bulla's books might be interesting to read; how he got ideas for his books; why writing a book takes a long time. Call attention to the titles Mr. Bulla has mentioned in his letter that are in your library collection. Encourage children to check with the public library for others. Distribute the Bulla bookmarks so children may check titles as you talk.

"Those of you who like horse stories will enjoy **A Ranch for Danny, Star of Wild Horse Canyon** and **Old Charlie.** Have you discovered his pirate story, **Pirate's Promise?** If you want your stories based on true happenings, read **John Billington, Friend of Squanto,** and **Squanto, Friend of the White Men.**"

"**Benito** is the story of a little orphan boy from Mexico who comes to live with his uncle in California. He has to work very hard and often he is lonely. One day he has a chance to go to town with his uncle. Here he meets a great artist. This meeting makes a great difference in his life. You'll be thrilled to discover how Benito made good in spite of his uncle."

"How did poppy seeds change a selfish old man into a good friend and neighbor? Read **The Poppy Seeds.**"

"Mr. Bulla has written several good stories about Indians. In **Eagle Feather,** playing around with Crook Nose's truck is very disastrous for the Indian boy, Eagle Feather. He must pay for the damage he has done. How can he do this? He wants to go to school, but he doesn't want to leave his family. What happens to make this wish come true?

"In the story, **Indian Hill,** we learn that being an Indian boy today isn't all fun. Kee and his mother find that living in a city is very different from life on the reservation. What happens to change their minds so that father can keep his job in the city, makes a good modern Indian story."

"We have found out many things about Mr. Bulla today, but we can still learn more by reading his books. In what part of the library will we look for them? How do we locate them on the shelf?"

Follow-up Activities:

Set a date for a Clyde Robert Bulla sharing period.

Suggest making questions which can be answered by titles or characters from these books.

Encourage the making of pictures, puppets, dolls, dioramas to motivate the reading of Bulla books by other library visitors.

USE OF RECORDINGS TO INTRODUCE AN AUTHOR

Purpose:

To acquaint children with books written by Emma Brock.

To share the fun of listening to **Here Comes Kristie.**

To learn how an author gathers material for a book.

Materials Needed:

The letter from Emma Brock in this manual.

A collection of the books by Emma Brock that your library has available.

The recording, "Here Comes Kristie," available from Sound Book Press Society, Inc., 36 Garth Rd., Scarsdale, N. Y. 10583. Order number: MSB60016.

Book jackets on the bulletin board to advertise the Brock collection.

Author information available from Alfred Knopf, Inc., 501 Madison Ave., New York, N. Y. 10022.

The Class Session:

"How would you get ready to be an author?" (Travel, study, do many things. Talk to people.)

"Emma Brock is a good example of a person who has done many of the things you have suggested. Her father was in the army, so the family traveled a great deal. She was born at Fort Shaw, Montana, in 1886. When she was two, the family moved to Fort Snelling, Minnesota. Later they were transferred to Colorado, to Illinois and back again to Montana. After she had finished going to school, she traveled in Europe. The letter she has written for us gives us an idea of the fun she has had doing her work."

Dear Boys and Girls:

Can you imagine me standing on a street corner with a yellow pencil in one hand and in the other a notebook about the size of typewriter paper? I would be making sketches of the buildings and of the people and animals.

Sometimes there would be a group of children and grown-ups watching me draw. Later I used a smaller sketchbook to be less conspicuous—even one the size of a folded dollar bill!

That is the way I collected material for the picture books I did of Brittany and Holland and Austria and the Black Forest in Germany.

Afterward I would make up a story about the people and what they would be doing. Then I would draw pictures for the illustrations from the sketches I had made in that country.

You can imagine how much fun it has been. Sometimes sketching ducks or geese or pigs in a farmyard. Or a donkey cart going to market to sell produce. Or a man cutting hay with a long scythe, or a woman washing clothes in a river.

That is the way I have done the books and I have enjoyed doing them so much, more than I can tell. And I hope you are enjoying them too.

Maybe I can draw a duck, but as you can plainly see, I make mistakes on the typewriter!

Sincerely, your friend,
EMMA L. BROCK

"Today we're going to listen to one of Emma Brock's stories, "Here Comes Kristie." Two boys, Elmer and Einar, wanted a horse so badly. They saved money and finally were able to buy what their father described as 'a sort of a kind of a horse.' From then on their troubles began."

After playing the record, discuss the difficulties they had with Kristie. See if they think Kristie was worth the money they spent for her.

The Second Class Session:

"Last time we talked about Emma Brock and how she got ready to be an author. Where in our FICTION section would we find her books?"

There are several other books that she has written which you will enjoy as much as we did "Here Comes Kristie."

Kristie's Buttercup tells how much Mother wants a Holstein cow. Father gives one-half of last year's corn money; the hired man adds his gold piece; the twins trade little K. Kristie likes the cow and is able to find her when she gets lost.

Come Along, Fish! has good storm pictures. Three Cornish fishermen are out in a bad storm at sea. They lose their nets. Good luck is with them, for they get them back again. How?

Kristie and the Colt is a collection of stories. The first one tells how Elmer and Einar get a little colt for their birthdays and how much they want Kristie to make friends with little K. The other stories: "Cake for Katie," "Peder's Gull," "Helping Hilda," and "Taking Care of Nellie" are fun to read because each of them has a surprise in it.

Drusilla is a good pioneer story. It tells about the exciting adventures of a cornhusk doll as she comes by covered wagon to Minnesota. The Indians, the gophers and Aunt Polly's cooking have much to do with her trip.

Kristie Goes to the Fair relates more problems with Kristie's hat. The greedy pig, Rosalie, eats it. Now what can they do? How will they get to the fair?

Plug Horse Derby will tell you of two horse races—one in which the magic word "oats" helped make a winner; another in which a horse's appetite made him lose the race. How does it feel to be a celebrity and have people ask you for your autograph and have your picture in the paper? You'll get some ideas from reading this book.

Remember we said that Emma Brock did much traveling? **At Midsummer Time** tells of a festival in Sweden and the experiences of Sigrid and her twin brother and sister, Kari and Nils. If you'd like to read about trolls, here's a book to take along.

Topsy-Turvy Family is another good pioneer story. You'll know why it has such a title after you have read of all their exciting experiences with Indians, animals and storms.

Three Ring Circus describes the experiences of a girl who decided she wanted to be a circus performer and must start her training at once. Did you ever get your heel hooked behind your ear? Sally did, and she couldn't get it down. She had many other problems, too, before she changed her mind.

If you ever tried to take pictures with your camera, you know how often you cut off heads, get the house and not the people, forget to get your thumb out of the way. Mary had all these problems and more, but she had good luck, too. Read **Mary's Camera** to find out what she did.

Follow-up Activities:

Set an Emma Brock Day for discussion of what has been read by the class and the sharing of any activities that have been carried out.

Other authors of interest to this grade level may be introduced by use of recordings: Miriam Mason's **Middle Sister** is available.

Books giving biographical information about authors:

The Story Behind Modern Books by Elizabeth Rider Montgomery. Dodd, Mead, 1949.
The Story Behind Great Stories by Elizabeth Rider Montgomery. Dodd, Mead, 1947.
Junior Book of Authors
More Junior Authors

Keep a file of magazine articles from such sources as:

Elementary English
Horn Book
Saturday Review
Sunday Book Supplements

FAIRY TALES

Purpose:

To acquaint children with the fairy tale section of the library.

To stimulate an interest in reading fairy tales.

To increase children's imagination.

Materials Needed:

Reference Material:

"Folk Tales Around the World," reprinted from COMPTON'S PICTURED ENCY-CLOPEDIA. F. E. Compton and Company, 1000 North Dearborn St., Chicago, Ill.

Fairy Tale Collections:

Arbuthnot, May Hill	TIME FOR FAIRY TALES. Scott
Association for Childhood Education International	TOLD UNDER THE GREEN UMBRELLA. Macmillan
Brooke, L. Leslie	THE GOLDEN GOOSE BOOK. Warne
Fenner, Phyllis R.	PRINCESSES AND PEASANT BOYS. Knopf
Hutchinson, Veronica	CANDLE-LIGHT STORIES. Putnam
	CHIMNEY CORNER FAIRY TALES. Putnam
	CHIMNEY CORNER STORIES. Putnam
Manning-Sanders, Ruth	A BOOK OF DWARFS. Dutton
	A BOOK OF GIANTS. Dutton
Rackham, Arthur	ARTHUR RACKHAM FAIRY BOOK. Lippincott
Rojankovsky, Feodor	THE TALL BOOK OF NURSERY TALES. Harper

Reading Record Booklet:

One for each member of the class. See page 80.

Collection of books listed on the reading record on display or markers placed in the books on the shelves.

The Class Session:

(Note three approaches following the introduction to the fairy tale section of the library.)

Arrange a reading circle facing the fairy tale section.

"In the nonfiction section of the library there are many smaller sections where books about the same topic are grouped together on the shelves. Today we are facing the section in which you will find fairy tales. All the books in this section do not have fairies or little winged creatures in them. In the beginning the word fairy meant "enchantment" to go by means of a story to another world where strange things may happen. Very often these stories do have tiny creatures in them that we know as fairies."

"Most of the stories in this section of the library could be called folk tales or the stories that have passed from generation to generation through storytelling. Mothers and fathers told the stories to their children and when their children grew up they told them to their own children. The stories were first told so long ago that no one knows when they were first told. Some people think that some stories are several thousand years old."

Approach No. 1:

"Another mystery is why or how some fairy tales or folk tales are so much alike. Some fairy tales seem to be several stories mixed together. In the story I will read to you, listen for similars or parts of the story that are like other stories you know."

"Another interesting thing about fairy stories is the rule of three. Things happen in threes. There may be three sisters, or three brothers, or things happen at the end of three days, or someone gets three wishes or three choices. As I read the story, 'Billy Beg and His Bull,' listen for the rule of three."

Read "Billy Beg and His Bull," CHIMNEY CORNER FAIRY STORIES.

"Did you hear any similars or parts of the story like another story you know?" (The story has a part in it something like "Cinderella" only the shoe is tried on men and boys. Billy Beg uses a stick and a cloth which reminds us of "The Lad Who Went to the North Wind.")

"Did you discover the rule of three in this story?" (The Queen was ill for three days. The henwife said her cure would be three mouthfuls of the blood of Billy Beg's bull. Billy's bull fights three bulls. Billy is hired to care for three goats, three cows, three horses, and three donkeys. Billy kills three giants.)

"Do you think the princess made a wise choice when she chose Billy Beg for her husband? Why? Why did she not choose the warrior? (Wise choices are made in fairy tales by wise people. The hero comes out on top and the wicked or dishonest get their just punishment.) "There are some very good stories in this section of the library. I call them 'too good to miss.' They are listed in this little booklet. Each of you may have a booklet to use as your reading list. As you finish reading the story, make a little checkmark on the line beside the title. Do you suppose someone in your class will read all of them?"

"On the cover of your booklet you will find the number that matches the number on the back of a fairy tale book. If you are looking for this section in the library, this number will guide you to the right place."

"Our library has two main parts. We have found many interesting books in the fiction section. This large part (point out the limits) is called the nonfiction section. Each book in this part of the library has a number on the back. This number is used along with the letter below the number to place the book in its proper place on the shelf. The number on a book of fairy tales is 398. This number is on the cover of your reading record booklet. Each book in the nonfiction section of the library has its special place and if you are looking at a book and decide you do not want to check it out or if you only want to use it during the library period, you must be careful to put it back in its proper place on the shelf."

> Demonstrate several ways the exact spot may be marked. The child may use his reading record booklet or a marker made of construction paper to slip into the place from which he has removed the book. The book just before the one taken from the shelf may be turned on end to mark the place. The two books on each side of the one being removed from the shelf may be slipped out over the shelf a bit. Some children may be able to determine the correct place for a book by first checking the number on the book spine, locating books with corresponding numbers on the shelf, checking the letter beneath the number and placing the book in alphabetical order in the proper section.

_____ Snow White and Rose Red

_____ Snow White and the Seven Dwarfs

_____ Stone Soup

_____ The Story of the Three Bears

_____ The Story of the Three Little Pigs

_____ This Is the House That Jack Built

_____ Three Billy Goats Gruff

_____ The Three Little Pigs

_____ The Three Wishes

_____ The Traveling Musicians

_____ Tom Tit Tot

_____ Tom, Tom, the Piper's Son

_____ When the Mississippi Was Wild

_____ The Wolf and the Seven Little Kids

Name _____

FAIRY TALES

_____ Aesop's Fables

_____ Baboushka and the Three Kings

_____ The Blind Men and the Elephant

_____ Cinderella

_____ Dame Wiggins of Lee and Her Seven Wonderful Cats

_____ The Fisherman and His Wife

_____ Gone Is Gone

_____ The Good-for-nothings

_____ The Hare and the Tortoise

_____ John Henry

_____ Journey Cake, Ho!

_____ The Lion and the Rat

_____ The Miller, His Son, and Their Donkey

_____ The Mitten

_____ My Mother Is the Most Beautiful Woman in the World

_____ Nibble Nibble Mousekin

_____ The North Wind and the Sun

_____ Old Mother Hubbard and Her Dog

_____ Old Woman and Her Pig

_____ Once a Mouse

_____ Puss in Boots

_____ Rapunzel

_____ Salt

_____ The Shoemaker and the Elves

_____ Six Foolish Fishermen

_____ The Sleeping Beauty

Approach No. 2:

Fairy tales come from all parts of the world. They are stories people told to entertain or to make work more fun.

Materials Needed:

The fairy tale books compiled by Virginia Haviland with titles beginning, FAVORITE FAIRY TALES TOLD IN . . .

A globe.

A reading record booklet for each member of the class: "Around the World on a Magic Carpet." Inside the folder a list of the fairy tale books compiled by Virginia Haviland listed by country.

The Class Session:

"Virginia Haviland is a librarian who is interested in fairy tales from countries all around the world. She has compiled or put together favorite stories from many countries and has had them made into separate books with the name of the country in the title."

Hold several books before the class, pointing out the titles.

"A long time ago, when these stories were first told, there were no jet planes, not even fast trains, or even cars. So, if people imagined getting someplace in a hurry, they had to do it by magic, with seven-league boots, or on the back of the wind. A favorite way to get places quickly by magic was on a flying carpet. I have a reading record booklet for each of you called, "Around the World on a Magic Carpet." During this coming week see how many countries you can visit by riding a magic carpet—reading a book. As you finish reading a book, make a check mark beside the title on your reading record. How many countries can you visit in a week?"

"Right now let's hop aboard our magic carpet and take a trip to _____."
(Select a favorite story to read or tell.)

81

Approach No. 3:

Fairy Tale—Picture Books. Outstanding illustrators of books for boys and girls have illustrated favorite fairy tales.

Materials Needed:

Fairy tale books illustrated by Marcia Brown:

CINDERELLA. Scribner (Caldecott Award Book)

DICK WHITTINGTON AND HIS CAT. Scribner

THE FLYING CARPET. Scribner

ONCE A MOUSE. Scribner (Caldecott Award Book)

PUSS IN BOOTS. Scribner

THE THREE BILLY GOATS GRUFF. Harcourt

STONE SOUP. Scribner

Biographical material and picture of Marcia Brown from Charles Scribner's Sons, 597 Fifth Ave., New York, N. Y. 10017.

"Miss Marcia Brown's Day," by Mary F. Kersting. **Elementary English.** Vol. XXXIII, No. 3, March 1956. pp. 131-141.

Filmstrips:

FS 48 THE THREE BILLY GOATS GRUFF. Weston Woods Studio

FS 7 STONE SOUP. Weston Woods Studio

The Class Session:

Present a bit of biographical information about Marcia Brown so the children will be aware of her love for reading and the library, and the importance of drawing, painting and writing in her life.

Examine several books illustrated by Marcia Brown. The children have noted similarities in artists' styles. Lead them to discover the variety in style and techniques used by Marcia Brown.

Use the filmstrips for THE THREE BILLY GOATS GRUFF, and STONE SOUP. After reading the story along with the filmstrip, go through the filmstrip, commenting on illustrations and encouraging remarks from the children.

Read the stories and include questions and remarks about the illustrations in the discussion period following. Guide children in discovering how exactly right Marcia Brown's illustrations are for the story. Note how unsuited the type of illustrations for CINDERELLA would be for STONE SOUP.

Call attention to the two Caldecott Award books, CINDERELLA and ONCE A MOUSE.

Can the children recognize the wood grain in the wood block prints in ONCE A MOUSE?

Do they see the illustrations are very different in the two books? How do they guess the illustrations were made for CINDERELLA?

Follow-up Activities:

Experimenting with watercolor.

Experimenting with block printing and discovering that a separate block is needed for printing each color used.

Look for books other than fairy tales illustrated by Marcia Brown. Find books written and illustrated by Marcia Brown.

Enjoy books illustrated by other well-known illustrators of books for boys and girls.

MORE FAMOUS ILLUSTRATORS AND THE FAIRY TALE BOOKS THEY HAVE ILLUSTRATED:

Adams, Adrienne	SNOW WHITE AND ROSE RED. Scribner
Anglund, Joan Walsh	NIBBLE NIBBLE MOUSEKIN. Harcourt
Artzybasheff, Boris	AESOP'S FABLES. Viking
Brooke, L. Leslie	THE GOLDEN GOOSE BOOK. Warne
	THE HOUSE IN THE WOOD. Warne
	THE STORY OF THE THREE BEARS. Warne
	THE STORY OF THE THREE LITTLE PIGS. Warne
Cooney, Barbara	THE LITTLE JUGGLER. Hastings House
DeAngeli, Marguerite	THE GOOSE GIRL. Doubleday
Duvoisin, Roger	THE MILLER, HIS SON, AND THEIR DONKEY. McGraw
Fischer, Hans	THE GOOD-FOR-NOTHINGS. Harcourt
	PUSS IN BOOTS. Harcourt
	THE TRAVELING MUSICIANS. Harcourt
Gag, Wanda	GONE IS GONE. Coward-McCann
	SNOW WHITE AND THE SEVEN DWARFS. Coward-McCann
	THREE GAY TALES FROM GRIMM. Coward-McCann
Galdone, Paul	THE BLIND MEN AND THE ELEPHANT. McGraw
	THE HARE AND THE TORTOISE. McGraw
	THE HOUSE THAT JACK BUILT. McGraw
	OLD MOTHER HUBBARD AND HER DOG. McGraw
	OLD WOMAN AND HER PIG. McGraw
	THE THREE WISHES. McGraw
	TOM, TOM, THE PIPER'S SON. McGraw
Hoffmann, Felix	RAPUNZEL. Harcourt
	THE SEVEN RAVENS. Harcourt
	THE SLEEPING BEAUTY. Harcourt
	THE WOLF AND THE SEVEN LITTLE KIDS. Harcourt
Keats, Ezra Jack	JOHN HENRY. Pantheon
McCloskey, Robert	JOURNEY CAKE, HO! Viking
Ness, Evaline	TOM TIT TOT. Scribner
Rackham, Arthur	ARTHUR RACKHAM FAIRY BOOK. Lippincott
Rojankovsky, Feodor	THE TALL BOOK OF NURSERY TALES. Harper
Sidjakov, Nicolas	BABOUSHKA AND THE THREE KINGS (Caldecott Award Book). Parnassus Press
Wildsmith, Brian	THE LION AND THE RAT. Watts
	THE NORTH WIND AND THE SUN. Watts

FAIRY AND FOLK TALE BOOKS SELECTED FOR THIRD GRADE READERS:

The following lists may suggest other approaches to presenting the fairy tale section of the library:

Countries of the World:

AFRICA:

Aardema, Verna	TALES FROM THE STORY HAT. Coward-McCann
Fournier, Catharine	THE COCONUT THIEVES. Scribner
Rickert, Edith	THE BOJABI TREE. Doubleday

ARABIA:

Brown, Marcia	THE FLYING CARPET. Scribner

BURMA:

Merrill, Jean	HIGH, WIDE AND HANDSOME. Young Scott
	SHAN'S LUCKY KNIFE. Scott

CZECHOSLOVAKIA:

Gag, Wanda	GONE IS GONE. Coward-McCann
Fillmore, Parker	THE SHEPHERD'S NOSEGAY. Harcourt

DENMARK:

Hatch, Mary C.	MORE DANISH TALES. Harcourt
	13 DANISH TALES. Harcourt

ENGLAND:

Brown, Marcia	DICK WHITTINGTON AND HIS CAT. Scribner
Ness, Evaline	TOM TIT TOT. Scribner

FINLAND:

Bowman, James C.	SEVEN SILLY WISE MEN. Whitman
Fillmore, Parker	THE SHEPHERD'S NOSEGAY. Harcourt

FRANCE:

Brown, Marcia	STONE SOUP. Scribner
Cooney, Barbara	THE LITTLE JUGGLER. Hastings House
Fischer, Hans	PUSS IN BOOTS. Harcourt
Perrault, Charles	CINDERELLA. Scribner
	PUSS IN BOOTS. Scribner
Todd, Mary Fidelis	THE JUGGLER OF NOTRE DAME. McGraw

GERMANY:

Anglund, Joan W.	NIBBLE NIBBLE MOUSEKIN. Harcourt
DeAngeli, Marguerite	THE GOOSE GIRL. Doubleday
Grimm, Jacob and Wilhelm	THE FISHERMAN AND HIS WIFE. Pantheon
	THE GOOD-FOR-NOTHINGS. Harcourt
	THE HOUSE IN THE WOOD. Warne
	RAPUNZEL. Harcourt
	THE SEVEN RAVENS. Harcourt
	THE SHOEMAKER AND THE ELVES. Scribner
	THE SLEEPING BEAUTY. Harcourt
	SNOW WHITE AND ROSE RED. Scribner
	SNOW WHITE AND THE SEVEN DWARFS. Coward-McCann
	THREE GAY TALES FROM GRIMM. Coward-McCann
	THE TRAVELING MUSICIANS. Harcourt
	THE WOLF AND THE SEVEN LITTLE KIDS. Harcourt

INDIA AND PAKISTAN:

Brown, Marcia	ONCE A MOUSE. Scribner
Quigley, Lillian	THE BLIND MEN AND THE ELEPHANT. Scribner
Saxe, John Godfrey	THE BLIND MEN AND THE ELEPHANT. McGraw
Siddiqui, Ashraf	TOONTOONY PIE. World

JAPAN:

Hodges, Margaret	THE WAVE. Houghton
Stamm, Claus	THREE STRONG WOMEN. Viking
	THE VERY SPECIAL BADGERS. Viking
Uchida, Yoshiko	THE DANCING KETTLE. Harcourt
	THE MAGIC LISTENING CAP. Harcourt

NORWAY:

Asbjornsen, Peter C. and Joren Moe	THE THREE BILLY GOATS GRUFF. Harcourt

POLAND:

Fournier, Catharine	THE GOLDEN SEED. Scribner

RUSSIA:

Reyher, Becky	MY MOTHER IS THE MOST BEAUTIFUL WOMAN IN THE WORLD. Lathrop
Robbins, Ruth	BABOUSHKA AND THE THREE KINGS. Parnassus Press
Tresselt, Alvin	THE MITTEN. Lathrop
Zemach, Harve	SALT. Follett

SWEDEN:

Zemach, Harve	NAIL SOUP. Follett

UNITED STATES OF AMERICA:

Chase, Richard	JACK AND THE THREE SILLIES. Houghton
Cothran, Jean	WITH A WIG, WITH A WAG. McKay
Harris, Joel C.	BRER RABBIT, adapted by Margaret Wise Brown. Harper
Keats, Ezra Jack	JOHN HENRY. Pantheon
LeGrand	WHEN THE MISSISSIPPI WAS WILD. Abingdon
Sawyer, Ruth	JOURNEY CAKE, HO! Viking

INDIANS OF NORTH AMERICA:

Belting, Natalia	THE LONG-TAILED BEAR, AND OTHER INDIAN LEGENDS. Bobbs
Curry, Jane Louise	DOWN FROM THE LOVELY MOUNTAIN, California Indian Tales. Harcourt
Macmillan, Cyrus	GLOOSKAP'S COUNTRY (Canada). Walck

Fables:

AESOP'S FABLES, wood engravings by Boris Artzybasheff, selected by Louis Untermeyer. Golden Press

THE HARE AND THE TORTOISE, pictures by Paul Galdone. McGraw

LaFontaine. THE LION AND THE RAT, illustrated by Brian Wildsmith. Watts

LaFontaine. THE NORTH WIND AND THE SUN, illustrated by Brian Wildsmith. Watts

THE MILLER, HIS SON, AND THEIR DONKEY, illustrated by Roger Duvoisin. McGraw

Participation:

"Say Along"—Stories easy to tell because of repeated phrases, cumulative pattern, rhyming.

DAME WIGGINS OF LEE AND HER SEVEN WONDERFUL CATS. McGraw

SIX FOOLISH FISHERMEN. Children's Press

THIS IS THE HOUSE THAT JACK BUILT. McGraw

OLD MOTHER HUBBARD AND HER DOG. McGraw

THE OLD WOMAN AND HER PIG. McGraw

THE STORY OF THE THREE BEARS. Warne

THE STORY OF THE THREE LITTLE PIGS. Warne

THE THREE LITTLE PIGS: in verse. Viking

THE THREE WISHES. McGraw

TOM, TOM, THE PIPER'S SON. McGraw

Follow-up Activities:

Creative dramatics. Have members of the class interpret a character from a fairy tale.
Puppet plays. Simple stick puppets or paper bag puppets make very effective characters for fairy tale productions.

Dramatization. Many folk tales or fairy tales lend themselves well to dramatization. Characterization is clear and the plot is straightforward.

A mural. The class or a committee may plan a mural around a theme such as the way characters from fairy tales travel. A mural may depict representations from the folk tales of a country. A mural based on favorite folk tales provides for a wide range of ideas.

Understanding people. When studying another country or another culture such as our American Indians, the folk tales can add enrichment and enjoyment to the unit.

Holidays. Special days and holidays such as Halloween, Christmas, and Easter are wonderful times to share with children folk tales relating to that special day. For example, at Halloween enjoy such old favorites as "The Hobyahs," "The Golden Arm," "Teeny Tiny," and "The Tinker and the Ghost."

THE LIBRARY'S SCIENCE SECTION

Purpose:

To introduce the science section of the library.

To provide children with a guide so they can find some of their own materials.

Materials Needed:

Prepare bookmarks for the class.

MY SCIENCE BOOKMARK

NAME ....

GRADE ....

500   SCIENCE

510   Mathematics

520   Astronomy (Stars, Planets, Moon)

530   Physics (Air, Electricity, Magnets, Machines)

540   Chemistry

550   Geology (Earth, Rocks, Minerals, Weather)

560   Paleontology (Dinosaurs, Fossils, Cavemen)

570   Biology (Living Things)

580   Botany (Plants)

590   Zoology (Animals)

Collect books from this section to be distributed to the reading tables.

The Class Session:

"Many times you have asked for books from the section we are going to explore today.

What topics in science have you been studying either in class or by yourself?"

Discuss these topics. List them on the board.

"I have made a bookmark for you to use as your guide."

Distribute the bookmarks. Talk about the number 500 and its meaning in the library. Examine each of the classes under the main number.

"Using your bookmark as a guide, let's see what number we would look under for the topics we have listed on the board."

Complete as many as possible, asking questions whenever necessary to clarify the headings.

"On each of your tables I have placed a collection of science books. They are arranged in order from 500 through 590. Notice that under each number is the letter which stands for the author's last name."

"Take time to examine the collection of books on your table, checking with your bookmark to see under which topic each one fits. Perhaps you'll find a science book to take with you this week."

Follow-up Activities:

Collect a group of books on a special topic in science to take back to the classroom.

Have children make a list by author and title of 5 science books on a special topic they would like to study.

Using their bookmarks as guides, have them practice finding science books on a particular topic or to answer a special question such as:

a. What color are a bluebird's eggs?

b. How large is a full-grown otter?

c. What causes hailstones to form?

d. What is a star?

e. Find a picture of poison ivy.

f. How can you prove that air takes up space?

Make a bulletin board display featuring a different science number each month.

Choose books such as these from your science collection to read to the class:

Starlings by Wilfred Bronson. Harcourt, Brace, 1948.

Elf Owl by Mary and Conrad Buff. Viking, 1958.

The Hole in the Tree by Jean George. Dutton, 1957.

Snow Tracks by Jean George. Dutton, 1958.

Elsa by Joy Adamson. Pantheon Books, 1961.

Possum by Robert M. McClung. Morrow, 1963.

Ruby Throat by Robert M. McClung. Morrow, 1950.

BIOGRAPHIES

Purpose:

To introduce biography as an interesting kind of reading.

To teach a simple way of locating a biography book.

Materials Needed:

Blackboard or chart paper.

A collection of easy-to-read biographies:

Childhood of Famous American Series.

Tablet paper.

The Class Session:

"I'm going to read to you a chapter from a special kind of book. As you listen, see if you can discover how it is different from the books you have been reading from the fiction and the easy section."

Chapters from these books are suggestions for the introduction of this lesson:

Howe, Jane Moore. **Amelia Earhart: Kansas Girl**, "Pioneers and Indians." Bobbs-Merrill. pp. 54-63.

Stevenson, Augusta. **Clara Barton: Girl Nurse**, "Smallpox!" Bobbs-Merrill. pp. 129-140.

Wilson, Ellen. **Ernie Pyle, Boy From Back Home**, "A Proud Moment." Bobbs-Merrill. pp. 115-125.

Whole books such as the following might be read as an introduction:

Dalgliesh, Alice. **Ride on the Wind** (Charles Lindbergh). Scribner's, 1956.

Lawson, Robert. **"They Were Strong and Good.** Viking, 1940.

After the reading see if the children can detect that what you have read is based on the life of a real person. When this has been established, continue with the discussion.

"Because this story is about the life of a real person, it is not placed in the easy or the fiction section, but is shelved with the NONFICTION in this part of our library."

Show clearly where this area is. Children may walk through the NONFICTION section. Assemble them in front of the biography books.

"These books are called BIOGRAPHIES. (Write this on the chart or board.) This interesting word comes from two Greek words—Bio meaning life, and Graphy meaning the process of writing. Together these two word parts tell us that a biography is the written account of someone's life."

"You are standing in front of the collection of biography books. These books tell us many fascinating things about the great men and women of the world. Perhaps one day we may find the story of your life in such a book. What kind of person would you have to be before such a book would be written about you?"

Discuss with them what makes a person famous.

Keep a list to use at next class session.

"I have collected a group of biographies for you to examine."

Place these on tables where they can gather about to make their choices.

"Next time we meet we will talk about your biographies and some of the interesting things you discovered. Write down on a slip of paper the name of your famous person and the number and letters from the spine of your book." (Show where the call number is.)

The Second Class Session:

"Did you get well acquainted with your new friend who went home with you the last time we met? What did you find out about this person that you think we would all like to know? How was the way your new friend lived different from the way you live? The last time you told me that a person was famous for these reasons: (Read from list you made with class during the last session.) Have you any new ideas after doing your reading? Why would you say that biographies are good books for us to know about?"

Lead them to discuss how such books help us understand other people; tell us about history; are as interesting as made-up stories; give us ideas for our own lives.

"Let's make a list of the famous people about whom you read."

After this is completed on the board or chart, explain how a biography book can be located.

"Each of you has a piece of paper on which you wrote the name of your famous person and the magic key which helps you find the book. Look at that magic key. Can anyone tell me what the two parts of that key mean?"

Ask the children what number was on the back of their books. When it is established that everyone has 92 or 921, whichever your library uses, see if they can reason that this number must stand for biographies.

"As I call the name of your famous person, tell me the magic key—the number and the letters—for which our special library name is CALL NUMBER. I will write it on our chart." The chart will look like this:

FAMOUS PERSON	CALL NUMBER

"We discovered that the number 92 or 921 stands for books that are biographies. Now who can tell us what the letters stand for that are below this number?"

If they cannot see this readily, have them go through the list of famous people with you as you underline the famous person's last name. Help them see that the famous person's last name gives us the two letters that go below the number.

"Who can explain to a new boy who might come to the library with you next time, just how to find a biography book on the shelf?" (Look for the 92's or the 921's in the Non-fiction Section. Find the first two letters of the famous person's last name. Check the title to be sure it is about the right person.)

"Today we are going to play a finding game. Each of you will be given a slip on which is written a famous person's name. You add the magic key: the CALL NUMBER. Show your slip to me when you are finished. If your CALL NUMBER is right, you may go to the shelves and see how well your magic key really works. When you locate your book, just pull it to the edge of the shelf and wait for me to check."

Follow-up Activities:

Make from tag board, strips (3″ x 8″); use these to make simulated spines for biographies of famous people that are generally familiar to a third grade student. Print on each spine the famous person's last name and the last name of the author. Leave the space for the call number blank. On construction paper slips (3″ x 4″), print the call numbers to go with them.

Give the spines to 15 students who will stand in front of the class; pass out one call number at a time to other members of the class. When 4 or 5 call numbers remain, give them out at one time. Children who held spines the first time may have a chance to match call numbers the next time.

Encourage students to read several biographies about the same person and compare the information.

When class activities point the way, help children make up lists of famous people such as inventors, explorers, sports heroes, nurses, authors, artists, musicians which they might find useful in their studies of science, social studies, art, health, literature, music, physical education.

POETRY

Purpose:

To acquaint children with the poetry section of the library.
To help them discover different kinds of poetry.

Materials Needed:

Read the preface from **Early Moon**, "A Short Talk on Poetry," by Carl Sandburg to prepare yourself for the poetry discussion.

Several poetry collections. The titles below are suggestions.

Arbuthnot, May Hill. **Time for Poetry.** Chicago: Scott, Foresman, 1961.

Chute, Marchete. **Around and About.** New York: E. P. Dutton Co., 1957.

O'Neill, Mary. **Hailstones and Halibut Bones.** New York: Doubleday, 1961.

Withers, Carl and Alta Jablow. **Rainbow in the Morning.** New York: Abelard-Schuman, 1961.

Blackboard or chart paper.

The Class Session:

"We have a special kind of book in our library which reminds me of going shopping. I can look through its pages, reading a little bit here and a longer bit there, finding old favorites, discovering new things, and finally finding just what I want to take with me. Such a book is a poetry book. Many of you have had the fun of going shopping for poetry. Can you tell us about a poem that you like very much? Have you learned some poems so that you can say them without the book? Why do you like to have your teacher read poems aloud to you?"

After a discussion of their favorites, recalling poems they have learned or those that they have enjoyed having read to them, call attention to the chart you have prepared on several kinds of poetry.

"There are many kinds of poetry. I have made a list of several which we are going to explore today.

From the board or chart, read the following ideas:

POETRY

1. Tells a story.
2. Paints a picture.
3. Makes us laugh.
4. Makes interesting sounds.
5. Describes our feelings.
6. Is used for games.
7. Makes us want to move in certain ways (rhythm).

"Let's listen to some poems that fit into these classes."

From TIME FOR POETRY read "Ballad of Johnny Appleseed" by Helmer O. Oleson, page 37, and "The Story of the Baby Squirrel" by Dorothy Aldis, page 56.

"Why are these called story poems? How could you write these stories in a different way? (Without rhyming words.)

"For the next poems, close your eyes and see what kind of pictures your imagination paints."

Read any of the color poems from HAILSTONES AND HALIBUT BONES." Discuss what they saw. Hopefully the color pictures will be very clear in their minds.

"Can you see how a writer with his words can do very much the same thing that an artist does with his paints?"

"We all like to laugh. Here are two jolly poems that are meant to cheer us up."

From TIME FOR POETRY read "The Pirate Don Dirk of Dowdee" by Mildred Plew Meigs, pages 133-134; and "There Once Was a Puffin" by Florence Page Jacques, pages 118-119.

"Poems are fun, too, because they make use of all kinds of sound effects. The same letter sound is repeated and sometimes strange new words are made up because they gave the poem an unusual rhythm."

Read from TIME FOR POETRY, "Three Little Puffins" by Eleanor Farjeon, page 119; and "I Was Once an Apple Pie" by Edward Lear, pages 97-99.

"There are other poems that describe very well just how we feel about people, things that happen to us, and our likes and dislikes."

Read from AROUND AND ABOUT, "Portrait," page 31; "Presents," page 36; "At Night," page 58; "My Dog," pages 16-17; "Drinking Fountain," pages 82-83.

"How many of you play jacks or jump rope? There are many jolly rhymes to use with these games and other games as well."

Read from RAINBOW IN THE MORNING, "Counting-Out Rhymes," "Skipping Rhymes" and "Spelling Rhymes." Children may wish to demonstrate how these rhymes are used in games.

"These poems will give you all a chance to take part. As I read, you make the motion that the rhythm or the beat of the poetry makes you feel."

Read from TIME FOR POETRY, "Elephants Walking" by Lenore M. Link, page 74 (heavy walk); "Hoppity" by A. A. Milne, page 94 (skipping); "Husky Hi" by Rose Fyleman, page 95 (galloping); "Mrs. Peck-Pigeon" by Eleanor Farjeon, page 52 (bobbing head).

Discuss the kinds of poetry they most enjoyed. Have them recall poems that they have heard before that fit into the categories you have been discussing.

"The poetry books in our library are easy to find because they are all together in one special part of the NONFICTION SECTION."

Assemble the class in the area where the poetry books are shelved. Explain the meaning of the large group number 800 for Literature. Show them several good collections as well as a variety by individual poets.

"Now when you come to the library and want to go shopping for poetry, remember to visit the Literature shelves with the 800 label above them."

Follow-up Activities:

Encourage children to make a collection of their favorite poems.

Compile a book of poems on a special topic such as weather or pets for the children to illustrate.

Suggest that each child prepare his favorite poem to read for the class.

Make tape recordings of poetry reading they have done.

Write poetry. Send class favorites to magazines such as HIGHLIGHTS, JACK AND JILL and the GOLDEN MAGAZINE which have a section devoted to junior authors.

Organize a group to do choral reading. LET'S-READ-TOGETHER POEMS compiled by Helen A. Brown and Harry J. Heltman, Row, Peterson, 1949, will give you suggestions for getting started on such a project.

INTRODUCING MAGAZINES

Purpose:

To introduce the library's magazine section.

To encourage regular reading of magazines for current information.

To acquaint children with the variety of materials to be found in magazines.

Materials Needed:

The magazines your library has available for the use of younger children (Highlights, Children's Digest, Golden Magazine, National Geographic School Bulletin, Jack and Jill).

Collections of back issues of these magazines for classroom use.

The Class Session:

"Our library has a section which we have not yet explored. This is our Magazine Section. What is the difference between a magazine and a book?"

Discuss their ideas. Help them to see that magazines are published at regular times; that they have many different kinds of materials in them; that since they are paperbound they need special care in handling. Point out the value of magazines for special day stories and articles. Call attention to the puzzles and caution against writing in magazines since this would spoil them for others. Tell them about continued stories and the fun of trying to guess what will happen before the next issue of the magazine comes.

"Highlights for Children is a magazine which has both fiction stories and nonfiction articles. (Give examples of both of these, reading one of each if time permits.) It also contains jokes and riddles which so many of you enjoy that we never have enough joke and riddle books to go around. (Read several of these.) There are good ideas for making useful things or playthings. (Show examples of these pages.) This magazine is an excellent one to share with your parents and your little brothers and sisters. One of its very special features is a page which you can help write." (Share several children's contributions from this page.)

The Golden Magazine has many of the same features as **Highlights.** Call attention to these in the same way the **Highlights** discussion was conducted. Stress the value of using magazines for up-to-date material in giving reports for classwork.

Use the same procedure for presenting the **Children's Digest** and **Jack and Jill.**

"For all of you boys and girls who like to find out about life in other countries, **The National Geographic School Bulletin** is a good place to start. It is published every week from September through May." (From several issues show the kinds of information that are available.)

"How many good reasons have we discovered for reading magazines?" (Up-to-date material; things to do for fun; good ideas to use for giving reports; how to make things in our spare time; good stories that can be read in a short time; pages of other children's writings where we may wish to send some of ours; jokes, riddles, and news for our sharing times at school; stories and poems to read to little brothers and sisters.)

"Magazines make worthwhile gifts because they keep coming all year. If a grandmother or an aunt asks what you would like for your birthday or for Christmas, this would make a good suggestion, for then you could do all the puzzles, cut out the paper dolls, use the monthly calendars, and have a source of pictures to clip for your scrapbooks or school assignments."

Explain the method used for checking out magazines used by your library.

Follow-up Activities:

Write stories and poems; draw pictures to send to magazines that conduct student participation pages.

Using back issues of magazines, make scrapbooks of articles, stories and poems on special topics.

Have a display of articles made from ideas given in magazines.

BIBLIOGRAPHY

Books for a Teacher's or Librarian's Collection:

Arbuthnot, May H. **Children and Books.** 3d ed. Chicago: Scott Foresman, 1964.

Arnstein, Flora J. **Poetry in the Elementary Classroom.** New York: Appleton-Century-Crofts, 1962.

Behavior Patterns in Children's Books, a bibliography compiled by Clara J. Kircher. Washington, D. C.: The Catholic University Press of America, 1966.

Curriculum for English. Poetry for the Elementary Grades. Champaign, Illinois: National Council of Teachers of English, 1966.

Freund, Roberta Bishop. **Open the Book.** New York: The Scarecrow Press, 1962.

Glaus, Marlene. **From Thoughts to Words.** Champaign, Illinois: The National Council of Teachers of English, 1965.

Haviland, Virginia. **Children's Literature, A Guide to Reference Sources.** Washington, D.C.: Library of Congress, 1966.

Huck, Charlotte S. and Doris A. Young. **Children's Literature in the Elementary School.** New York: Holt, Rinehart and Winston, 1961 (Book Reports pp. 402-407.)